SOCCER
Restart
PLAYS

J. Malcolm Simon, MA
New Jersey Institute of Technology

John A. Reeves, EdD
Columbia University

Human Kinetics Publishers

Library of Congress Cataloging-in-Publication Data

Simon, J. Malcolm.
    Soccer restart plays / J. Malcolm Simon, John A. Reeves.
      p. cm.
    ISBN 0-87322-521-X
    1. Soccer--Coaching.   I. Reeves, John A. (John Albert), 1939-   .
  II. Title.
  GV943.8.S56   1994
  796.334'07'7--dc20   93-24693
                                                                          CIP

ISBN: 0-87322-521-X

Photo on page 1 by Mike Drazdzinski, courtesy of University of Pittsburgh Sports Information; photo on page 71 courtesy of University of Wisconsin Women's Sports Information; photo on page 113 courtesy of Michigan State University Sports Information.

Acquisitions Editor: Brian Holding; Developmental Editor: Mary E. Fowler; Assistant Editors: Lisa Sotirelis, Ed Giles; Copyeditor: Chris Drews; Proofreader: Karen Dorman; Production Director: Ernie Noa; Typesetter: Sandra Meier; Text Design: Keith Blomberg; Text Layout: Tara Welsch; Cover Design: Jack Davis; Cover Photo: Mike Drazdzinski; Interior Art: Gretchen Walters, Keith Blomberg; Printer: Versa Press

Human Kinetics books are available at special discounts for bulk purchase for sales promotions, premiums, fund-raising, or educational use. Special editions or book excerpts can also be created to specification. For details, contact the Special Sales Manager at Human Kinetics.

Printed in the United States of America   10 9 8 7 6 5 4 3 2

Human Kinetics
P.O. Box 5076, Champaign, IL 61825-5076
1-800-747-4457

Canada: Human Kinetics, Box 24040, Windsor, ON N8Y 4Y9
1-800-465-7301 (in Canada only)

Europe: Human Kinetics, P.O. Box IW14, Leeds LS16 6TR, England
0532-781708

Australia: Human Kinetics, P.O. Box 80, Kingswood 5062, South Australia
618-374-0433

New Zealand: Human Kinetics, P.O. Box 105-231, Auckland 1
(09) 309-2259

To all the soccer players it has been our privilege to coach

CONTENTS

FOREWORD

My first reaction after reading *Soccer Restart Plays* was, Why hasn't anyone produced a book like this before? Mal Simon and John Reeves are to be congratulated for compiling the best set plays of many of the top coaches in the U.S. and England.

Each play is exquisitely diagrammed and expertly explained. The editors standardized and simplified the format so you can quickly refer to the play you need, be it a free kick, corner kick, throw-in, or kickoff. An added bonus is the insights coach contributors offer into strategies for using the plays.

Whether you coach soccer at the youth, high school, college, or even professional level, you're sure to find plays in this book that can give your team an important goal in a crucial match. The plays in *Soccer Restart Plays* were included because they work. They *score!*

If you doubt it, take this excellent book to the field with you for your next practice. Pick out the plays you believe might work for your team. Teach your players the procedures, using the coaching points provided. Then have them run the plays in the appropriate game situations. If you do, you'll see what this book has to offer. And you'll be a better coach.

Cliff McCrath
Seattle Pacific University

CONTRIBUTING COACHES

PREFACE

Goal! There is nothing more satisfying to a team's players and coaches, nor anything as exciting to its supporters, than a goal scored from a well-planned and well-executed restart play.

The importance of restart plays in the scoring of goals cannot be overemphasized. More than a third of all goals—and often the deciding goals—are scored from restarts. A restart play, especially from scoring vicinity, is always better than an aimless kick. Such opportunities are too valuable to waste.

Although soccer, unlike American football, is not a set-play type of game, every contest provides frequent opportunities to use set plays. When the action has stopped and a restart is needed to get the ball moving again, the play should be carefully planned and executed. *Soccer Restart Plays* will teach you how to achieve this end.

Soccer Restart Plays includes 68 plays and 48 variations for free kicks, corner kicks, throw-ins, and kickoffs solicited from successful high school and intercollegiate coaches throughout the United States and England. We also have included a few of our own favorites. The plays, organized in alphabetical order and clearly illustrated, are suitable for all skill levels. However, when selecting plays for teams at the lower skill levels, you may want to choose plays that require fewer passes or fewer players.

We have divided this book into three parts. Part I is devoted to free kicks. We explain the difference between direct and indirect free kicks, and refer to the NCAA rules for men's and women's soccer that indicate the offenses for which free kicks are awarded. You will learn how to deal with various defenses, and you will find 36 free kick plays and additional variations to help your team beat them.

Part II, on corner kicks, also lists the applicable rules and describes how to deal with numerous defenses. The 22 corner kick plays and variations will be a valuable offensive scoring resource.

Part III features the throw-in and the kickoff. The introduction again discusses the relevant rules and ways to counter numerous defenses. You will find 10 throw-in and kickoff restarts and additional variations to strengthen your play in these situations.

Soccer Restart Plays is unique in that it provides coaches with many restart plays that have withstood the test of time. Devoting significant practice time to restart plays seems not only logical but essential. Expect using this book to pay off in goals.

ACKNOWLEDGMENTS

We are grateful to the coaches who contributed to *Soccer Restart Plays* and to Kenneth Simon, a former outstanding soccer player at Glassboro State College, who suggested the need for such a book. We also thank Cliff McCrath, head coach at Seattle Pacific University and a valued contributor to our books, for his endorsement. Finally, it has been our pleasure to work with Human Kinetics Publishers on our four books; in particular, we thank Brian Holding for his guidance on our earlier books and Mary Fowler for her advice and patience on this book.

THE
FREE KICK

The best place to begin our presentation of restart plays is with a situation that gives the offense a high percentage of kicks that score—the free kick. Gaining a tactical advantage in the free kick situation takes proper positioning and quick thinking on the part of your offense. One of your biggest coaching challenges is to prepare your players to organize themselves efficiently for free kicks. Whether the shot at goal comes from a single player's direct attempt or involves two or three teammates, all of your players need to be ready to execute their roles.

In Part I we discuss free kick strategy. We give you tips for determining what plays to use in the particular situations you may face. Chapter 1 begins by distinguishing between direct and indirect free kicks. We look at the types of defenses your team might encounter and help you assess the defense by looking at its positioning to determine its strengths and weaknesses. Finally, to assist you in strategy formation, we provide an overview of attacking principles you can use when your team is awarded a free kick.

In chapter 2 you'll find 36 free kick plays used and designed by premier college and high school coaches. Many plays include variations, giving you additional options for attacking the goal. The helpful diagrams that accompany each play show you how to position players and sequence their movements so your team is sure to score!

Remember, in the heat of competition even experienced players can forget or ignore what they have learned. So have your team practice free kicks repeatedly under gamelike conditions. If you do, you'll reduce players' confusion and increase their confidence in achieving their goal. The following plays appear alphabetically in chapter 2. If your team is at a lower skill level, you may want to select plays that require fewer passes and fewer players.

APPLE'S DELIGHT

AROUND THE WALL

ATTACKING THE POST

BACK DOOR THE WALL

BLAST-OFF

BOYLER OPTIONS

CORTLAND

DELAY

DIRECTIONAL DECOYS

DOWN THE LINE

EITHER OR

FAKE AND CHIP

GHOST BEHIND THE WALL

GO AWAY

GOING FOR GOAL

HEEL

HIDDEN PLAYER

HOT FOOT

INDIRECT SCREEN

LINER COMBO
OFF THE WALL
OPEN PLAYER ON END OF
  WALL
OPTIONS
PENMEN SPECIAL
PLAYER ISOLATION
PULL
RUN OVER AND SHOOT
SHOOT THROUGH WALL
SPIN AND SHOOT
STRAIGHT SHOOTER
THREE-PLAYER COMBO
THROUGH THE GAP
THROUGH THE LEGS
TOXIC
TRIANGULAR SERIES
ULTRA CHALLENGE

CHAPTER 1

FREE KICK TACTICS

An offense taking a free kick has, percentage-wise, one of the best chances to score. A free kick is taken to resume play after play has been stopped by the referee for any of the rule violations listed in Table 1.

RULES FOR THE FREE KICK

 A *direct free kick* is one from which a goal can be scored directly from the initial kick.

 An *indirect free kick* is one from which a goal cannot be scored directly from the initial kick. The ball must be played or touched by a player other than the initial kicker before passing through the goal.

The free kick is taken by a member of the team against which the violation was committed. It is taken from the point where the violation occurred (unless otherwise specified in the rules).

When a free kick is being taken, defending players cannot be within 10 yards of the ball until it is in play, unless the defender is standing on his or her own goal line between the goalposts. The free kick is retaken if a player on the defending team is within 10 yards of the ball and intentionally interferes with the kick. Any player who tries to slow the game by not getting 10 yards from the ball is first cautioned; if the violation is repeated, the player may be ejected from the game.

As soon as the ball is in position to be played, the referee gives a signal, usually a whistle. The ball must be stationary when the kick

Table 1 Violations Resulting in Free Kicks

Violations that result in a direct free kick	Violations that result in an indirect free kick
Handling the ball	A player playing the ball a second time before it has been played by another player at the kickoff, on a throw-in, on a free kick, on a corner kick, on a goal kick (if the ball has passed outside the penalty area), or on a penalty kick
Holding an opponent	
Pushing an opponent	
Striking or attempting to strike an opponent	
Jumping at an opponent	
Kicking or attempting to kick an opponent	
Tripping or attempting to trip an opponent	The goalkeeper carrying the ball more than four steps
Using the knee on an opponent	The goalkeeper delaying getting rid of the ball
Charging an opponent violently or dangerously	A substitution or resubstitution being made at an improper time
Handling by the goalkeeper outside the penalty area	A substitution or resubstitution being made without reporting to the referee
Violently and intentionally fouling the goalkeeper while in possession of the ball in the penalty area	Persons other than the players and linesmen entering the field of play without the referee's permission
Goalkeeper intentionally striking or attempting to strike an opponent with the ball	Illegal coaching from the sidelines after previously being advised by the referee against a recurrence
Charging illegally when the ball is not within the playing distance, unless being obstructed	Dissenting by word or action with a referee's decision
Spitting at an opponent	Unsporting behavior
	Dangerous play
	To resume play after a player has been ejected from the game for misconduct, provided a separate violation has not been committed at the same time that requires a different restart
	Offside
	Charging illegally (not violent or dangerous)
	Interfering with the goalkeeper or impeding the goalkeeper in any manner until he or she releases the ball, or kicking or attempting to kick the ball when it is in the goalkeeper's possession

Table 1   *(continued)*

Violations that result in a direct free kick	Violations that result in an indirect free kick
	Illegal obstruction other than holding Player leaving the field of play during the progress of the game without the consent of the referee

Note. All direct kicks awarded to the offensive team in the penalty area are *penalty kicks.*

is taken and is not in play until it has traveled the distance of its circumference (27 inches). The ball may be kicked in any direction. The player who initiates the free kick may not play the ball again until it has been touched or played by another player.

Dealing With the Defense

Players defending against free kicks position themselves according to the location of the ball relative to the goal being attacked.

When your team is taking a free kick from the final third of the field, defenders will assume their positions immediately and a "wall" of two to five players (or perhaps more in a goal-line situation) will be formed. The primary purpose of the defenders' wall is to protect the near-post portion of their goal, which is most vulnerable. This enables the goalkeeper to protect the remainder of the goal. Usually, the goalkeeper or another defensive player gives instructions for forming the defensive wall. This defending player usually stands by the near post. He or she positions one defender on an imaginary line between the ball and the outside of the near post; then players form a wall by standing to the inside (relative to the post) of the first positioned player protecting the goal. The legs of the players in the wall probably will be close enough together to prohibit your team from kicking a ball between the players' legs. The closer to the goal that the free kick is taken, the more players you probably will encounter in the wall. Once the free kick has been taken and attacking from the field ensues, defending players will break from the wall to defend attacking players and space.

If your team is attacking in your defensive third of the field (nearest your own goal), the defense must guard your players *and* the space your players may occupy upon movement. Defenders generally position themselves between their own goal and whatever opponents they are marking. In this situation, defending players would not use a wall against a free kick.

The principles for defending free kicks taken in the middle third of the field are similar, but the defensive players will mark somewhat closer and they will assume defensive positions immediately to prevent a quick attack on goal. Figure 1 suggests the most common number of players in the wall depending upon the location of the ball relative to the goal.

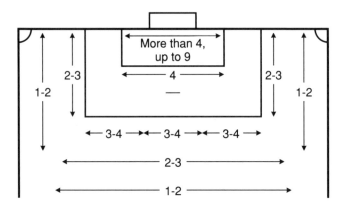

Figure 1.   The usual number of players in the wall, depending on where the ball is relative to the goal.

Attacking Principles

On free kicks the attacking team enjoys significant advantages:

- The team has possession of a stationary ball.
- No opponent may be within 10 yards of the ball until it is kicked.
- The offense may act quickly and score a goal while the defensive players are adjusting to the situation. Conversely, the offense has time to execute a well-practiced plan.
- A high percentage of goals are scored from free kicks.

After your team is awarded a free kick, its first priority should be to act fast to exploit existing defensive weaknesses. If the kick is direct, the defense is not set, and the free kick is awarded in the final attacking third of the field, this fast exploitation often means taking a shot on goal. There is no better set play than a direct shot on goal that has a reasonable chance of scoring.

If the defense is set, a designated offensive player signals—by word or physical action such as raising either hand—which well-rehearsed play is to be executed. More than one player should be assigned as the one to signal the play because the preferred designated player may be out of the game at the time.

Even though as few as one, two, or three players might touch the ball on a free kick restart, all attacking players have a role. Most attacking players, except the goalkeeper, will serve as decoys, who distract defensive players from the space needed for the play.

CHAPTER 2

FREE KICK PLAYS

Practice makes perfect. A few of the 36 plays that follow should be rehearsed thoroughly during practice so that play selection, signaling, and execution are precise in game play. As players practice, intent on improvement, their efforts will be rewarded when goals are scored from free kick restarts.

Usually the coach or a designated field player determines the play to be executed. Play selection is based on these variables:

- Whether the free kick is direct or indirect
- The distance from the goal being attacked
- The positions taken by the defenders
- Strengths and weaknesses of both attackers and defenders
- Environmental conditions (wet weather might suggest a hard shot to the goalkeeper, whose hands may be wet or who might slip; wind may prompt keeping the ball on the ground; sun may disturb the vision of the goalkeeper, suggesting a high lofted shot)

KEY TO PLAY DIAGRAMS

D = *Defender*   〜〜〜➔ **= Dribble**

G = *Goalkeeper*   ------➔ **= Pass**

                                      ·············➔ **= Shot**

                                        ————➔ **= Sprint**

                                        ⊛ **= Ball**

APPLE'S DELIGHT

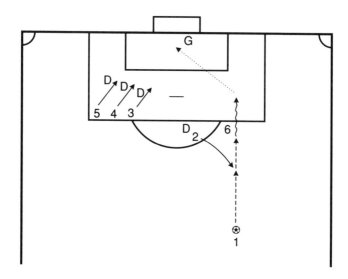

Formation

The ball is placed 40 to 50 yards from the goal and slightly to the right of the center circle. Attacker 1 is in position to take the free kick. Attacker 6 is straight ahead of 1, at the top of the penalty area. Attacker 2 is just inside the penalty-area restraining arc a few yards from 6. Attackers 3, 4, and 5 stand in a line along the left side of the 18-yard line.

Procedure

2 starts the play by moving toward the ball and calling for the pass. 1 makes a crisp pass to 2, who lets the ball run through to 6. 6 shields the ball from the defender, turns with the ball to the outside, and, after one or two touches, takes a shot to the far post. 3, 4, and 5 move to the goal to be in position for a possible rebound. One of these players must cover the far post.

CONTRIBUTOR: Stephen R. Locker, Men's Coach, Harvard University, Cambridge, Massachusetts

AROUND THE WALL

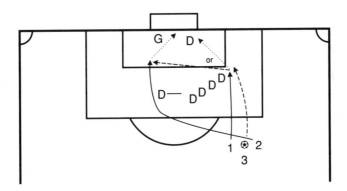

Formation
The ball is placed just outside the right side of the 18-yard line. Attackers 1, 2, and 3 are in position to take the free kick, standing equidistant from the ball to the left, right, and rear, respectively.

Procedure
1 runs across the ball to the right side of the defensive wall. Almost simultaneously, 2 cuts behind 1 and runs across the ball to the left side of the wall toward the far post. 3 passes to 1, who shoots on goal or hooks the ball back to the far post to 2, who shoots on goal.

CONTRIBUTOR: Manfred Schellscheidt, Men's Coach, Seton Hall University, South Orange, New Jersey

ATTACKING THE POST

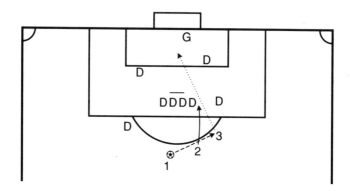

Formation

The ball is placed 10 yards outside the middle of the 18-yard line. Attacker 1 is in position to take the free kick. Attacker 2 is five yards to the right of 1, and Attacker 3 is five yards to the right of 2.

Procedure

2 runs toward the near-post end of the defensive wall. 1 passes to 3, who takes a first-time shot on goal.

Variation 1

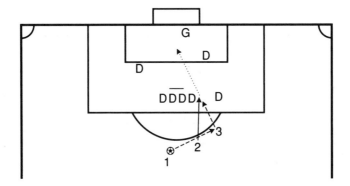

2 runs toward the near-post end of the defensive wall. 1 passes to 3. 3 passes to 2, who takes a first-time shot on goal or controls the ball and then takes a shot on goal.

Variation 2

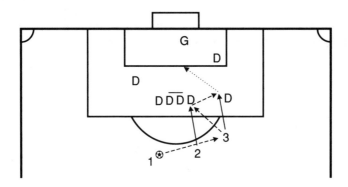

2 runs toward the near-post end of the defensive wall. 1 passes to 3. 3 passes to 2. 3 follows up the pass, receives a square pass from 2, and either takes a first-time shot on goal or controls the ball and takes a shot on goal.

CONTRIBUTOR: Gus Constantine, Men's Coach, New York University, New York, New York

BACK DOOR THE WALL

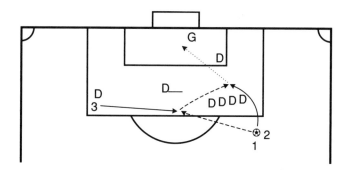

Formation

The ball is placed just outside the right corner of the penalty area. Attackers 1 and 2 are in position to take the free kick. Attacker 3 takes a weak-side position even with, and about 20 yards to the side of, the defensive wall.

Procedure

1 fakes a shot on goal and runs over the ball around the near-post side of the wall, staying onside. In rapid sequence, 2 passes to 3, who has made a timed run toward the wall, and 3 makes a one-touch pass behind the wall to 1, who takes a shot on goal.

CONTRIBUTOR: Jerry Yeagley, Men's Coach, Indiana University, Bloomington, Indiana

BLAST-OFF ▬▬▬▬▬▬▬▬▬▬▬▬▬▬▬▬▬▬▬▬▬

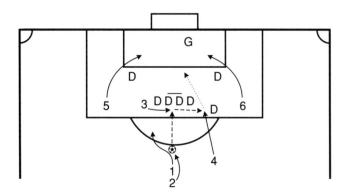

Formation
The ball is placed just outside the midpoint of the penalty-area restraining arc. Attackers 1 and 2 are in position to take the free kick. Attacker 3 stands slightly in front of the left end of the defensive wall. Attacker 4 is five yards to the right of 1. Attackers 5 and 6 are 10 yards to the left and right, respectively, of the defensive wall.

Procedure
1 runs as if to take a blast shot on goal but instead runs over the ball and off to the left. 2 follows 1 and takes a low, hard shot toward the defensive wall. 3, moving across in front of the wall, taps the ball to 4, who, after a momentary delay, moves to receive the pass and take a first-time shot on goal. 5 and 6 move to the post areas and stay alert for a possible rebound.

CONTRIBUTOR: J. Malcolm Simon, Director of Physical Education and Athletics, New Jersey Institute of Technology, Newark, New Jersey

BOYLER OPTIONS

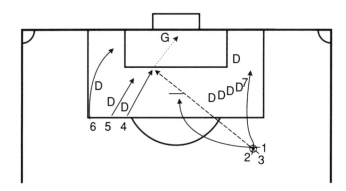

Formation

The ball is placed outside the right side of the 18-yard line. Attackers 1, 2, and 3 are in position to take the free kick. Attackers 4, 5, and 6 are in a line along the far left side of the 18-yard line. Attacker 7 stands at the near-post end of the defensive wall.

Procedure

In sequence, 1 runs over the ball and makes a curling run toward the penalty line, 2 runs over the ball and makes a straight run past 7 at the near-post end of the wall, and 4, 5, and 6 run toward the far post. 3 makes a lob pass to the far post, and either 4, 5, or 6 takes a one-time head shot on goal. The runs and pass must be timed to avoid players off the ball getting into offside positions.

Variation

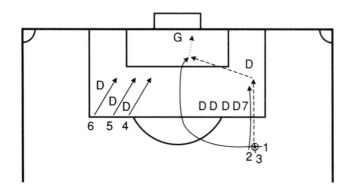

1 runs over the ball and makes a curling run toward the near post. 2 runs over the ball and makes a straight run past 7 at the near-post end of the defensive wall. 3 makes a ground pass to 2, who passes to 1 at the near post. As 2 passes to 1, Attackers 4, 5, and 6 sprint toward the goal area to be in position for a possible rebound. 1 takes a first-time shot on goal.

CONTRIBUTOR: Gavin Donaldson, Men's Coach, West Virginia Wesleyan College, Buckhannon, West Virginia

CORTLAND

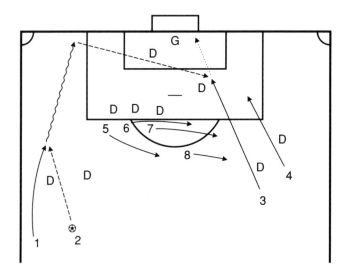

Formation
The ball is placed 50 yards from the goal line on the left side of the field. Attacker 2 is in position to take the free kick. Attacker 1 is behind and to the left of 2. Attackers 3 and 4 are on the opposite side of the field. Attackers 5, 6, 7, and 8 spread out in the middle of the field as far toward the goal as the defense allows.

Procedure
On a predetermined signal, 5, 6, 7, and 8 move away from the middle of the field in order to create space for 1, who is overlapping on the left side of the field. 2 passes the ball to 1. 1 takes the ball to the goal line and crosses to 3 and 4, who are sprinting toward the goal. The first player to contact the ball shoots on goal. 5, 6, 7, and 8 stay alert for a possible rebound or defensive clear.

CONTRIBUTOR: Chris J. Malone, Women's Coach, State University of New York College at Cortland, Cortland, New York

DELAY

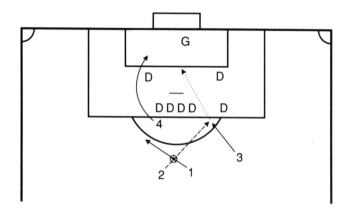

Formation
The ball is placed just outside the midpoint of the penalty-area re-straining arc. Attackers 1 and 2 are in position to take the free kick. Attacker 3 is 10 yards to the right and slightly forward of 1. Attacker 4 stands in front of the left end of the defensive wall.

Procedure
1 moves across the ball and off to the left side as 2 follows immediately with a direct pass to 3, who makes a delayed sprint forward to take a first-time shot on goal. 4 spins off the left end of the defensive wall to be ready for a possible rebound.

CONTRIBUTOR: J. Malcolm Simon, Director of Physical Education and Athletics, New Jersey Institute of Technology, Newark, New Jersey

DIRECTIONAL DECOYS

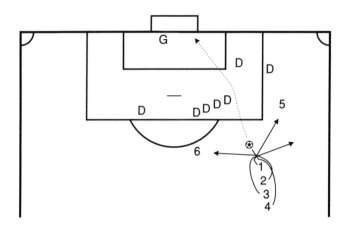

Formation

The ball is placed outside the right side of the 18-yard line. Attacker 1 is in position to take the free kick. Attackers 2, 3, and 4 stand in a line directly behind 1. Attackers 5 and 6 stand five yards to the right and left, respectively, of the ball.

Procedure

A direct shot on goal around the near end of the wall is taken by the player in the line who has been designated by an onfield decision by the four players or by a number or letter signal called out by the coach. The nonshooters each run over the ball and break alternately to the left and right of the defensive wall. The direction of the shot will be determined by the setup of the wall and the position of the goalkeeper.

Variation

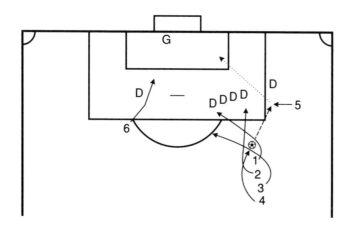

Instead of taking a shot on goal, the designated player passes to 5, who runs toward the ball to receive the pass. 5 either takes a first-time shot on goal or dribbles into a better position and then takes a shot on goal. 6 runs toward the goal to be in position for a possible rebound.

CONTRIBUTOR: Daniel R. Coombs, Boys' Coach, Loyola Academy, Willmette, Illinois; Girls' Coach, Mother McAuley High School, Chicago, Illinois

DOWN THE LINE

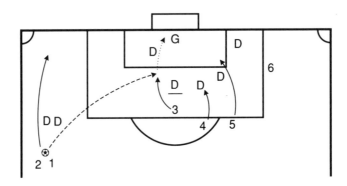

Formation
The ball is placed on either side of the field outside the penalty box. Attackers 1 and 2 are in position to take the free kick. Attackers 3, 4, and 5 stand in an arc across the far side of the penalty area. Attacker 6 stands outside the far sideline of the penalty area.

Procedure
1 runs over the ball and continues down the line. 2 passes the ball into the penalty area. On the pass, 3, 4, and 5 make diagonal runs into the penalty area toward the direction of the pass. The first player to contact the ball takes a first-time shot on goal while the other players keep alert for a possible rebound or pass. 6 stays outside the penalty area, alert for a long rebound or attempted clear by the defense.

Variation

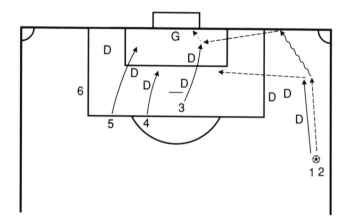

1 runs over the ball and continues down the line. 2 passes down the line to 1. 1 makes a first-time pass to the goal area or dribbles the ball to the goal line and passes to either the near or far post. 3, 4, and 5 make timed runs toward the direction of either pass. The first player to contact the ball takes a first-time shot on goal while the other players keep alert for a possible rebound or pass. 6 stays outside the penalty area, alert for a long rebound or attempted clear.

CONTRIBUTOR: Alan R. Kirkup, Women's Coach, Southern Methodist University, Dallas, Texas

EITHER OR

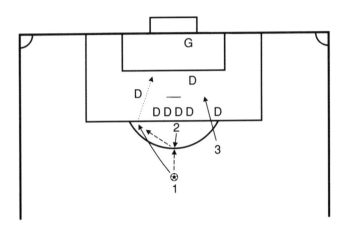

Formation
The ball is placed outside the midpoint of the penalty-area restraining arc. Attacker 1 is in position to take the free kick. Attacker 2 stands in front of the middle of the defensive wall. Attacker 3 is 10 yards to the right of 1 and halfway between 1 and 2.

Procedure
As 1 moves to take the kick, 2 moves toward the ball. 1 passes forward to 2. After the pass, 1 immediately moves to the left and receives a pass back from 2. 1 takes a first-time shot on goal. 3 moves to the post to be alert for a possible rebound. If defensive attention is concentrated on 1 and 2, 1 makes a diagonal pass to 3, who moves to the post and takes a first-time shot on goal.

CONTRIBUTOR: J. Malcolm Simon, Director of Physical Education and Athletics, New Jersey Institute of Technology, Newark, New Jersey

FAKE AND CHIP

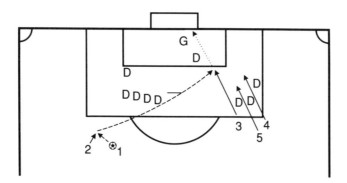

Formation

The ball is placed just outside the left side of the penalty area. Attackers 1 and 2 are in position to take the free kick to the right and left of the ball, respectively. Attackers 3, 4, and 5 are a few feet apart from each other outside the right side of the penalty area.

Procedure

The ball is played from 1 to 2 as if for a shot by 2 around the wall. Instead, 2 chips the ball to the far post for 3, 4, and 5, who are simultaneously running toward the goal. Whoever contacts the ball takes a first-time shot on goal, and the other players continue toward goal to be in position for a possible rebound.

CONTRIBUTOR: Mike Getman, Men's Coach, University of Alabama at Birmingham, Birmingham, Alabama

GHOST BEHIND THE WALL ━━━━━━

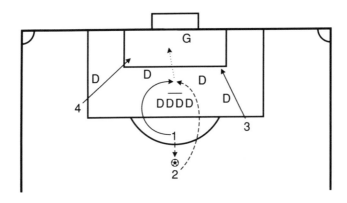

Formation
The ball is placed just outside the midpoint of the penalty-area re-straining arc. Attacker 1 stands with one foot on the ball, facing Attacker 2, who stands one yard behind the ball. Attackers 3 and 4 stand 15 yards to the right and left, respectively, of the wall.

Procedure
On a prearranged signal, 1 rolls the ball to 2. Immediately after the pass, 1 makes a curling run around the wall. 2 makes a chip pass over the wall for 1 to control and shoot on goal. 3 and 4 make timed runs to the post areas to be in position for a possible rebound.

Variation

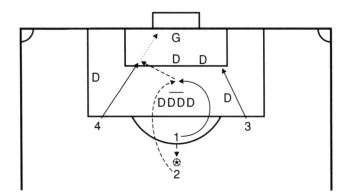

On a prearranged signal, 1 rolls the ball back to 2. Immediately after the pass, 1 makes a curling run around the wall. 2 makes a chip pass over the wall for 1 to control. 1 passes to either 3 or 4, who shoots on goal.

CONTRIBUTOR: Stephen G. Scullion, Boys' Coach, Folling Community Club, Pynce and Wear, England

GO AWAY

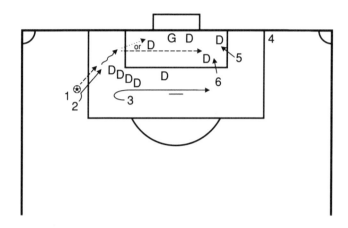

Formation
The ball is placed outside the left side of the penalty area. Attackers 1 and 2 are in position to take the free kick. Attacker 3 stands a few yards in front of the right side of the defensive wall. Attackers 5 and 6 stand a few yards apart just outside the right corner of the goal area. Attacker 4 stands outside the penalty area near the goal line on the right side of the field.

Procedure
3 starts to move toward the ball and is waved away from the play by 1. 3 turns and moves toward 6. 2 runs over the ball and continues toward the near-post end of the defensive wall. 1 steps as if to make a chip pass over the wall but instead passes on the ground to 2. 2 shields and dribbles the ball around the wall, then either shoots on goal or passes toward the far post to 5 and 6. Whoever contacts the ball shoots on goal.

CONTRIBUTOR: Harry S. Fleishman, Boys' Coach, Shady Side Academy, Pittsburgh, Pennsylvania

GOING FOR GOAL

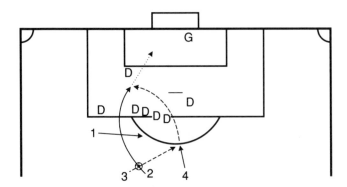

Formation
The ball is placed 30 yards from the goal line just to the left of the penalty-area restraining arc. Attackers 2 and 3 are in position to take the free kick. Attacker 4 stands about five yards to the right of the ball and about five yards in front of the defensive wall. Attacker 1 stands five yards in front of and to the left of the ball.

Procedure
This play is particularly effective against close defensive marking. 1 sprints toward the middle of the field, parallel to the 18-yard line. 2 sprints over the ball toward the area vacated by 1 and continues past the far-post end of the defensive wall. 3 passes the ball to 4, who makes a one-touch pass to 2. 2 shoots on goal.

CONTRIBUTOR: Gene Chyzowych, Boys' Coach, Columbia High School, Maplewood, New Jersey

HEEL

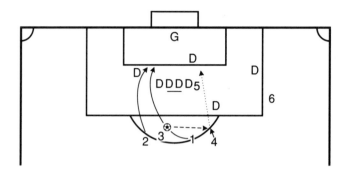

Formation
The ball is placed just outside the midpoint of the 18-yard line. Attacker 3 is in position to take the free kick. Attacker 2 stands about three yards to the left of 3. Attacker 1 stands about two yards to the right of 3 with Attacker 4 about two yards farther to the right. Attacker 5 stands at the right end of the defensive wall. Attacker 6 stands just outside the right side of the penalty area.

Procedure
1 sprints over the ball toward the left end of the defensive wall. 2 sprints around 1. 3, after faking to 1 and 2, heels the ball to 4 who takes a first-time shot on goal. 1 and 2 sprint toward the goal to be in position for a possible rebound.

Variation 1

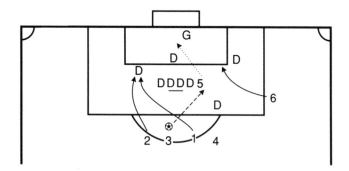

Following the initial sprints off the ball by 1 and 2, 3 passes to the outside of 5, who turns and shoots on goal. 1, 2, and 6 sprint toward goal to be in position for a possible rebound.

Variation 2

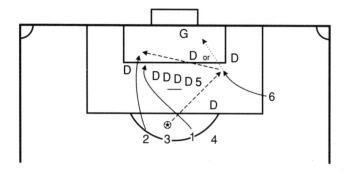

Following the initial sprints off the ball by 1 and 2, 3 makes a chip pass to 6, who has sprinted toward the goal area. 6 takes a first-time shot on goal or passes across the goal to 1 and 2, who have sprinted toward the goal area. Whoever contacts the ball shoots on goal.

CONTRIBUTOR: Wayne A. Mones, Men's Coach, Western Connecticut State University, Danbury, Connecticut

HIDDEN PLAYER

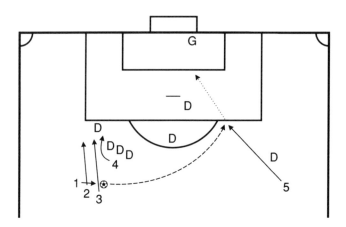

Formation
The ball is placed outside the left side of the 18-yard line. Attackers 1, 2, and 3 are in position to take the free kick. Attacker 4 stands in front of the defensive wall. Attacker 5—the "hidden player," who must be deceptive, fast, and a solid kicker—stands on the right side of the field square with the ball.

Procedure
2 and 3 explosively sprint toward the left side of the defensive wall. 4 moves to the near-post end of the defensive wall. 1 strikes the ball toward the right side of the penalty area to 5, who has cut inside the defender and run toward the 18-yard line. 5 takes a first-time shot on goal.

CONTRIBUTOR: Raul A. Donoso, Boys' Coach, Irvington High School, Irvington, New Jersey

HOT FOOT ▬▬▬▬▬▬▬▬▬▬▬

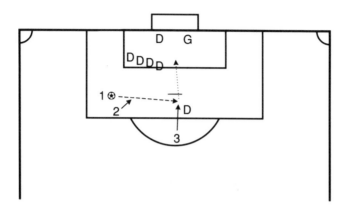

Formation
The ball is placed inside the left side of the penalty area, 15 yards from the goal line. Attacker 1 stands to the left of the ball in position to take the free kick. Attacker 2 is one yard behind and to the right of the ball. Attacker 3 stands on the midpoint of the penalty-area restraining arc.

Procedure
2 runs diagonally forward. 1 passes to 2 as 3 simultaneously runs forward. 2 lets the ball run through to 3, who either takes a first-time shot on goal or dribbles to evade a defender and then shoots on goal.

CONTRIBUTOR: Nick Kvasic, Men's Coach, College of Staten Island, Staten Island, New York

INDIRECT SCREEN

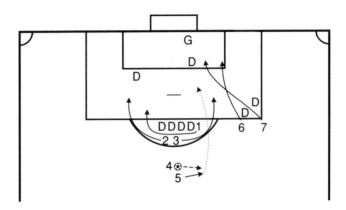

Formation
The ball is placed 10 yards outside the middle of the 18-yard line. Attackers 4 and 5 are in position to take the free kick, with 5 facing the defensive wall and 4 standing to the left of and facing the ball. Attackers 2 and 3, both facing the ball, stand close together between the ball and the defensive wall to obstruct the defenders' view of the ball. Attacker 1 stands at the right end of the wall. Attackers 6 and 7 stand at the top of the right side of the 18-yard line.

Procedure
1 initiates the play by running across the front of the defensive wall and breaking toward the near post. 4 makes a push pass sideways for 5, who has timed a run to take a one-touch swerving shot on goal around the end of the wall vacated by 1. To be in position for a possible rebound, 6 runs toward the far post, 7 runs toward the goalkeeper, and 2 and 3 break opposite each other and run toward the goal.

Variation

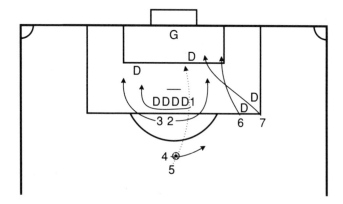

1 initiates the play by running across the front of the defensive wall and breaking toward the near post. If the wall is poorly set up, 4 runs over the ball and 5 takes a direct shot on goal. To be in position for a possible rebound, 6 runs toward the far post, 7 runs toward the goalkeeper, and 2 and 3 break opposite each other and run toward the goal.

CONTRIBUTOR: Michelle C. Morgan, Women's Coach, Amherst College, Amherst, Massachusetts

LINER COMBO

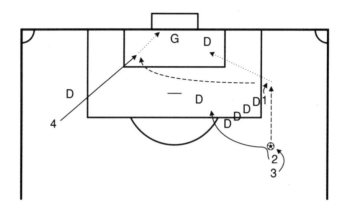

Formation
The ball is placed 10 yards outside the right side of the 18-yard line. Attacker 2 is in position to take the free kick. Attacker 3 stands directly behind 2. Attacker 1 is at the end of the near-post side of the defensive wall. Attacker 4 is 10 yards outside the left side of the 18-yard line.

Procedure
2 runs over the ball and past the far-post side of the defensive wall. 3 passes the ball straight down the line to the outside of 1. 1 turns just as the ball passes by and either takes a shot on goal or crosses to 4, who has made a timed run to the far post to be in position for a possible pass and first-time shot on goal.

Variation 1

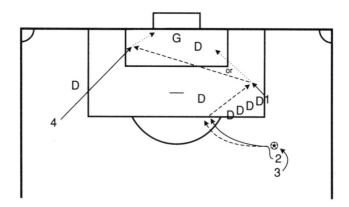

2 runs over the ball and past the far-post side of the defensive wall. 3 passes to the outside of 2, who makes a one-touch wall pass behind the defensive wall to 1. 1 shoots on goal or crosses to 4, who has made a timed run to the far post to be in position for a possible pass and first-time shot on goal.

Variation 2

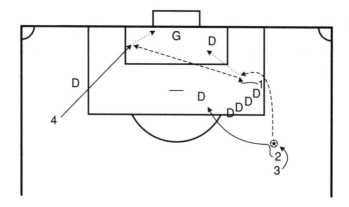

2 runs over the ball and past the far-post side of the defensive wall. 3 makes a chip pass over the wall to 1, who runs behind the wall as soon as the ball is passed. The intent of 2's run is to draw a defender from behind the wall, creating space for 1. 1 shoots on goal or passes to 4, who has made a timed run to the far post to be in position for a possible pass and first-time shot on goal.

CONTRIBUTOR: William J. Viger, Boys' Coach, Wheeler High School, Marietta, Georgia

OFF THE WALL

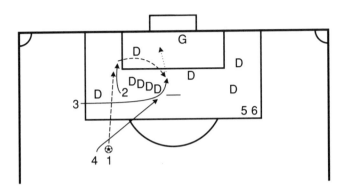

Formation
The ball is placed a few yards outside the left side of the 18-yard line. Attackers 1 and 4 are in position to take the free kick. Attacker 2 is standing at the near-post end of the defensive wall. Attacker 3, as a decoy, stands 10 yards in front and to the left of 4. Attackers 5 and 6 are at the right side of the penalty area.

Procedure
3 sprints toward the penalty line. 4 runs over the ball toward the penalty line. If the defender moves with 3, 1 plays the ball on the ground to the side of 2. 2, whose back is to the wall to shield the ball from those players, follows the ball as it runs on and makes a cross to the penalty line for either 3 or 4 to shoot on goal.

Variation 1

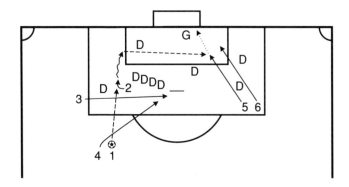

3 sprints toward the penalty line. 4 runs over the ball toward the penalty line. If the defender moves with 3, 1 plays the ball on the ground to the side of 2. 2 dribbles the ball toward the goal line and crosses to the far post to 5 and 6, who have run toward the goal area. Whoever contacts the ball shoots on goal.

Variation 2

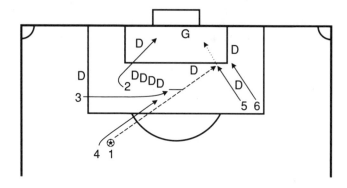

3 sprints toward the penalty line. 4 runs over the ball toward the penalty line. If the defender does not follow 3, 1 plays the ball to the far post to 5 and 6, who have run toward the goal area. Whoever contacts the ball shoots on goal. 2 follows the pass to the goal to be in position for a possible rebound.

CONTRIBUTOR: David W. Wright, Men's Coach, Gettysburg College, Gettysburg, Pennsylvania

OPEN PLAYER ON END OF WALL ━━━━

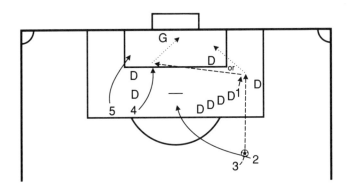

Formation

The ball is placed 10 yards outside the right side of the 18-yard line. Attackers 2 and 3 are in position to take the free kick. Attacker 1 is at the near-post end of the defensive wall. Attackers 4 and 5 stand on the left side of the penalty area.

Procedure

If 1 is free, the play is on. 2 runs over the ball toward the penalty line to draw attention. 3 sends a crisp, rolling ball ahead of 1. 1 must turn and, within two or three steps, strike the ball low on goal to the near post or pass it in the air to the far post for 4 and 5, who are crashing to the far-post area. Whoever contacts the ball shoots on goal.

Variation

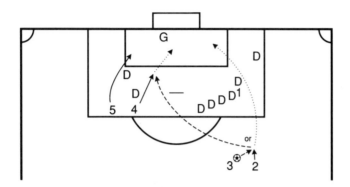

If 1 is marked, 3 rolls the ball to 2, who shoots on goal or makes a chip pass to the far post for 4 or 5, who makes a head shot on goal.

CONTRIBUTOR: Loren E. Kline, Men's Coach, University of Delaware, Newark, Delaware

OPTIONS

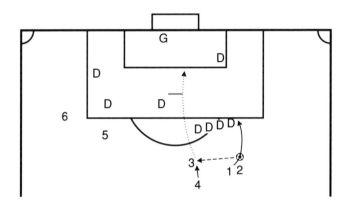

Formation
The ball is placed outside the right side of the 18-yard line. Attackers 1 and 2 are in position to take the free kick. Attacker 3 is five yards to the left of the ball. Attacker 4 is directly behind 3. Attackers 5 and 6 stand outside the left side of the penalty area.

Procedure
1 runs over the ball toward the near-post end of the defensive wall. 2 passes square to 3, who stops the ball for 4, who shoots directly on goal.

Variation 1

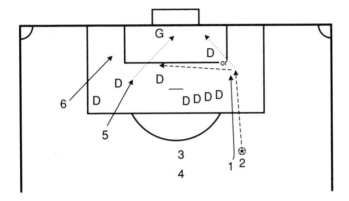

1 runs over the ball and past the near-post end of the defensive wall. 2 plays the ball wide to 1. 1 shoots on goal or passes to 5 and 6, who have run toward the far post. Whoever contacts the ball shoots on goal.

Variation 2

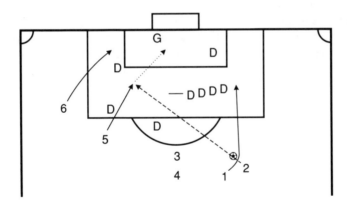

1 runs over the ball toward the near-post end of the defensive wall. 2 passes to 5 or 6, who have made wide runs toward the far post. Whoever contacts the ball shoots on goal.

CONTRIBUTOR: Jim Felix, Assistant Men's Coach, Harvard University, Cambridge, Massachusetts

PENMEN SPECIAL

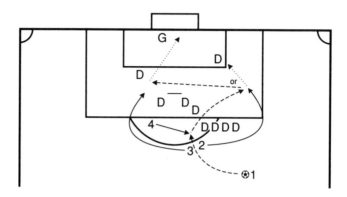

Formation
The ball is placed 10 yards outside the right side of the 18-yard line. Attacker 1 is in position to take the free kick. Attackers 2 and 3 are to the left side and slightly in front of the defensive wall. Attacker 4 is 10 yards to the left of the far-post end of the defensive wall.

Procedure
2 walks toward the near-post end of the defensive wall. As 2 reaches the end of the wall, 3 makes a curling run toward the far post. 4 checks toward 1. 1 plays the ball to 4. 4 makes a one-touch pass to 2, who began to run behind the wall as soon as the first pass was made. 2 shoots on goal or passes to 3, who shoots on goal.

Variation 1

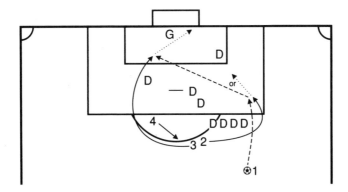

2 walks toward the near-post end of the defensive wall. As 2 reaches the end of the wall, 3 makes a curling run toward the far post. 4 checks toward 1. 1 makes a chip pass over the wall to 2, who shoots on goal or passes toward the far post to 3, who shoots on goal.

Variation 2

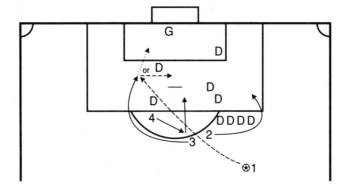

2 walks toward the near-post end of the defensive wall. As 2 reaches the end of the wall, 3 makes a curling run toward the far post. 4 checks toward 1. 1 makes a chip pass over the wall to the far post to 3. 3 takes a first-time shot on goal or passes to 2 and 4, who have run toward the goal area to be in position for a possible pass and shot on goal.

CONTRIBUTOR: John T. Rootes, Men's Coach, New Hampshire College, Manchester, New Hampshire

PLAYER ISOLATION

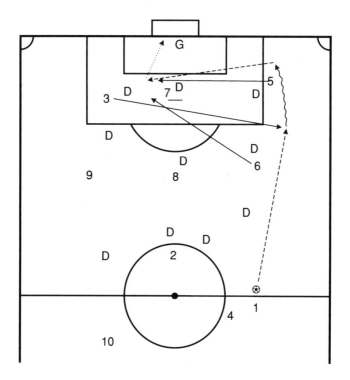

Formation

The ball is placed at midfield on the right side of the field. Attacker 1 is in position to take the free kick. Attacker 4 is a few yards behind and to the left of 1. Attacker 2 is at the top of the center circle in the attacking half of the field. Most of the remaining attackers are spread throughout the attacking half of the field with Attacker 3, the target player, in the left side of the penalty area.

Procedure

5 and 6 attempt to take their defenders out of the passing lane of 1 by running toward 3. 3 runs toward the area vacated by 5 and 6 and receives a pass from 1. 3 carries the ball down the wing and crosses it to 5 or 6 on the opposite side of the field. The first player to contact the ball takes a first-time shot on goal.

Variation 1

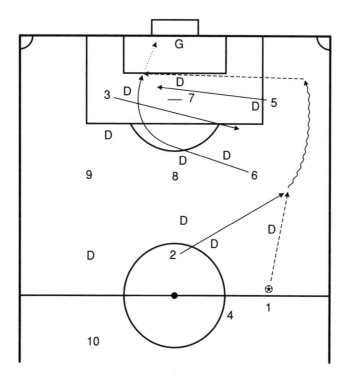

5 and 6 take their defenders out of the passing lane of 1 by running toward 3. 3 runs toward the area vacated by 5 and 6. 2 moves forward to the right, receives a pass from 1, and carries the ball down the wing to cross to 5, 6, or 7. The first player to contact the ball takes a first-time shot on goal.

Variation 2

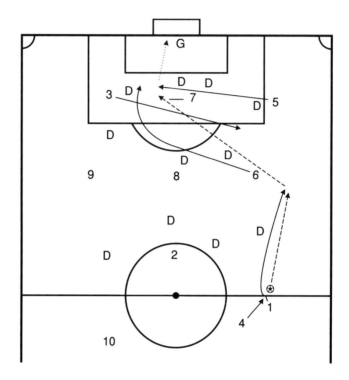

5 and 6 take their defenders out of the passing lane of 1 by running toward 3. 3 runs toward the area vacated by 5 and 6. 1 fakes a pass and runs over the ball. 4 moves to the ball and touches it down the line to 1, who crosses it to 5, 6, or 7. The first player to contact the ball takes a first-time shot on goal.

CONTRIBUTOR: Larry M. Gross, Women's Coach, North Carolina State University, Raleigh, North Carolina

PULL

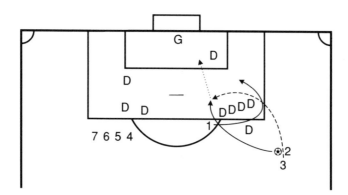

Formation
The ball is placed outside the right side of the 18-yard line and 25 yards from the goal line. Attackers 2 and 3 are in position to take the free kick. Attacker 1 stands at the far-post end of the defensive wall. Attackers 4, 5, 6, and 7 stand in a line on the left side of the 18-yard line.

Procedure
On a prearranged signal, 1 sprints around the front of the defensive wall and then toward the near post. At the same time 2 sprints over the ball and past the far-post end of the wall. 3 makes a chip pass over the wall to either 1 or 2, who shoots on goal. 4, 5, 6, and 7 create space for 1 and 2 by maintaining their positions and keeping their defenders' attention on them.

CONTRIBUTOR: Bob Winch, Assistant Men's Coach, Clemson University, Clemson, South Carolina

RUN OVER AND SHOOT

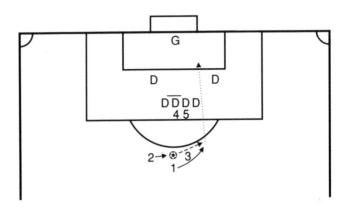

Formation
The ball is placed outside the middle of the 18-yard line. Attackers 1, 2, and 3 are in position to take the free kick. Attackers 4 and 5 stand in front of the defensive wall facing the ball.

Procedure
2 rolls the ball between 3's legs while 1 moves forward and to the right to take a shot on goal around the wall. The shot can be taken toward either post depending on the setup of the defensive wall and the position of the goalkeeper. 4 and 5 maintain their positions to obstruct the defenders' view.

Variation 1

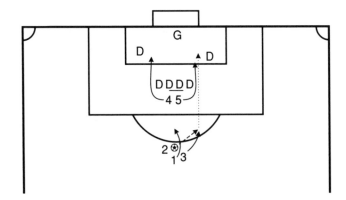

1 runs over the ball. 3 runs forward and to the right. 2 passes to 3, who shoots on goal. 4 and 5 curl off opposite ends of the defensive wall before the shot and sprint to the goal to be in position for a possible rebound.

Variation 2

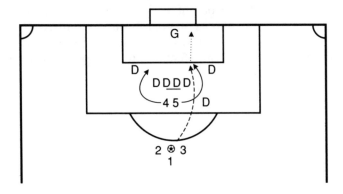

4 and 5 curl around opposite ends of the defensive wall. 1 chips the ball over the wall to 4 or 5. Whoever contacts the ball shoots on goal, and the other player follows up for a possible rebound.

CONTRIBUTOR: Robert G. Reasso, Men's Coach, Rutgers University, Piscataway, New Jersey

SHOOT THROUGH WALL ━━━━━━━━━

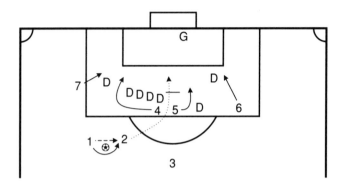

Formation
The ball is placed just outside the left side of the 18-yard line. Attacker 1 is in position to take the free kick. Attacker 2 is a yard to the right of the ball. Attacker 3 is 10 yards to the right of the ball. Attackers 4 and 5 are to the right and slightly in front of the far-post end of the defensive wall. Attackers 6 and 7 are about 10 yards to the right and left, respectively, of the defensive wall.

Procedure
1 taps the ball to 2. 2 controls the ball with a sole-of-the-foot trap. 1 follows up the pass and shoots on goal through the offensive wall set up by 4 and 5. 4, 5, 6, and 7 follow up the shot on goal to be in position for a possible rebound. 1, 2, and 3 maintain their positions to be ready for a possible long rebound.

Variation 1

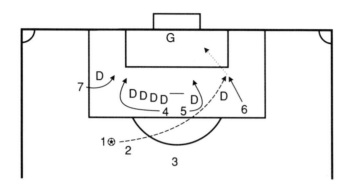

1 makes a chip pass to 6, who sprints toward the far post and shoots on goal. 4, 5, and 7 follow up the shot to be in position for a possible rebound.

Variation 2

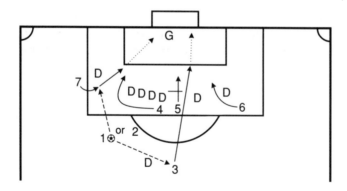

1 passes to either 3 or 7, who sprints toward the goal area and shoots on goal. 4, 5, and 6 follow up the shot to be in position for a possible rebound.

CONTRIBUTOR: Keith D. Tabatznik, Men's Coach, Georgetown University, Washington, DC

SPIN AND SHOOT

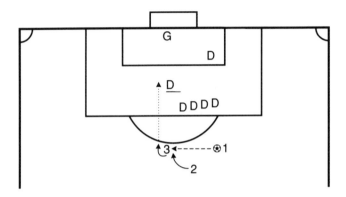

Formation
The ball is placed just outside the right side of the penalty-area restraining arc. Attacker 1 is in position to take the free kick. Attacker 3 is five yards to the left of 1. Attacker 2 is a few yards behind and to the left of 1.

Procedure
1 passes to 3, who stops the ball with a sole-of-the-foot trap. 2 sprints toward the ball as if to take a shot on goal. 3 holds the ball to commit the defense to block the shot. 3 then spins outside with the ball and takes a left-footed shot on goal.

Variation

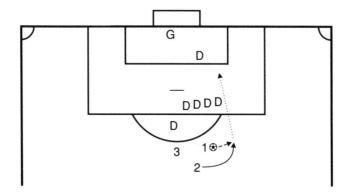

1 backheels the ball to 2, who runs behind 1 and takes a right-footed shot on goal around the near-post end of the defensive wall.

CONTRIBUTOR: Gary R. Parsons, Men's Coach, Oakland University, Rochester, Michigan

STRAIGHT SHOOTER ▬▬▬▬▬▬▬▬

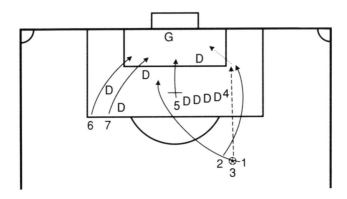

Formation
The ball is placed 10 yards outside the right side of the 18-yard line. Attackers 1, 2, and 3 are in position to take the free kick. Attackers 4 and 5 stand on opposite ends of the defensive wall. Attackers 6 and 7 stand just outside the left side of the 18-yard line.

Procedure
1 runs over the ball and around the far-post end of the defensive wall. 2 runs over the ball and around 4 at the near-post end of the defensive wall. 3 plays the ball firmly on the ground to 2, timing the pass so that the ball and 2 arrive at the same time in the area behind and to the right of the near-post end of the defensive wall. 2 takes a first-time shot on goal. 4 holds a firm position, to screen the end defensive player, until the pass is made. 5, 6, and 7, who moved into the goal area immediately after the pass, follow up the shot on goal to be in position for a possible rebound.

Variation

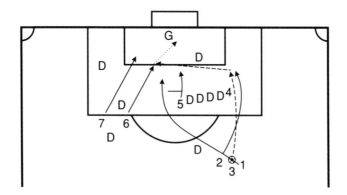

1 runs over the ball and around the far-post end of the defensive wall. 2 runs over the ball and around 4 at the near-post end of the defensive wall. 3 plays the ball firmly on the ground to 2, timing the pass so that the ball and 2 arrive at the same time in the area behind and to the right of the near-post end of the defensive wall. If a reasonable shot is not possible, 2 plays the ball across the goal mouth toward 5, 6, and 7, who moved into the goal area immediately after the pass. Whoever contacts the ball shoots on goal.

CONTRIBUTOR: Joseph A. Amorim, Men's Coach, Haverford College, Haverford, Pennsylvania

THREE-PLAYER COMBO

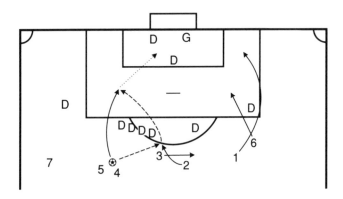

Formation

The ball is placed 15 yards outside the left side of the 18-yard line. Attackers 4 and 5 are in position to take the free kick. Attackers 3, 2, 1, and 6 line up to the right of the ball from left to right, respectively, in staggered positions. 7 stands to the left of the ball near the sideline.

Procedure

4 runs over the ball toward the near-post end of the defensive wall. 2 and 3 switch positions. 6 slowly runs toward the middle of the penalty area while 1 loops around 6 toward the far post. 5 passes to 2, who makes a first-time pass behind the defensive wall to 4, who has run past the near-post end of the wall to meet the ball. 4 takes a shot on goal. 1 and 6 stay alert for a possible rebound.

Variation

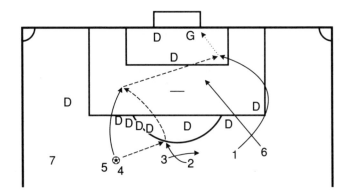

4 runs over the ball toward the near-post end of the defensive wall. 2 and 3 switch positions. 6 slowly runs toward the middle of the penalty area while 1 loops around 6 toward the far post. 5 passes to 2, who makes a first-time pass behind the defensive wall to 4, who has run past the near-post end of the wall to meet the pass. 4 passes to 1 at the far post. 1 shoots on goal. 6 stays alert for a possible rebound.

CONTRIBUTOR: Bob A. Dikranian, Assistant Men's Coach, Southern Connecticut State University, New Haven, Connecticut

THROUGH THE GAP

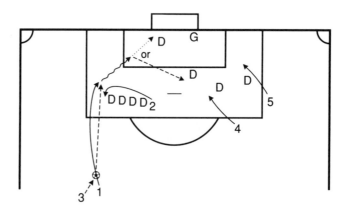

Formation
The ball is placed 10 yards outside the left side of the 18-yard line. Attackers 1 and 3 are in position to take the free kick. Attacker 2 stands at the far-post end of the defensive wall. Attackers 4 and 5 stand just outside the right side of the penalty area.

Procedure
1 runs over the ball and stops just outside the near-post end of the defensive wall. Simultaneously, 2 moves behind the wall to a position off the shoulder of the defender at the near-post end of the wall. 3 then passes the ball through the gap created by 1 and 2. 1 moves with the ball and either shoots on goal or passes to 4 or 5, who are sprinting toward the goal. Whoever contacts the ball shoots on goal.

CONTRIBUTOR: Sigi Schmid, Men's Coach, University of California, Los Angeles, Los Angeles, California

THROUGH THE LEGS

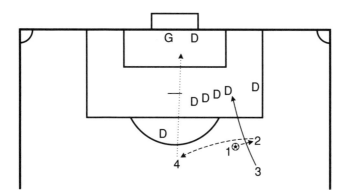

Formation
The ball is placed 5 yards outside the right side of the 18-yard line. Attackers 1, 2, and 3 are in position to take the free kick, with 2 to the right of 1 and 3 a few yards farther away from goal and behind 2. 4 stands about 10 yards to the left of and a little behind 1.

Procedure
1 rolls the ball to 2, who stops it. 3 runs over the ball toward the defensive wall. 2 passes the ball, through the legs of 1, to 4, who takes a first-time shot on goal.

CONTRIBUTOR: Andy Jennings, Men's Soccer Coach, Vassar College, Poughkeepsie, New York

TOXIC

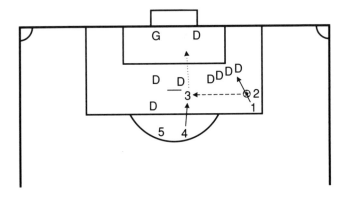

Formation
The ball is placed just inside the extreme right side of the 18-yard line. Attackers 1 and 2 are in position to take the free kick. Attacker 3 stands 10 yards to the left of the ball. Attacker 4 stands a few yards farther away from the goal and behind 3. Attacker 5 stands a few yards to the left of 4.

Procedure
1 runs over the ball toward the defensive wall. 2 immediately passes the ball to 3. 3 stops the ball with a sole-of-the-foot trap. 4 moves forward quickly and takes a shot on goal. Although the shot can be to either post, a near-post shot is preferable if the ball has been passed quickly enough to beat the angle of the defensive wall and if the goalkeeper is covering the far post.

Variation

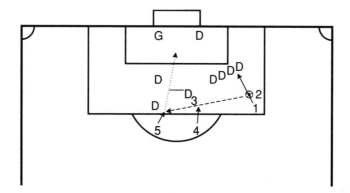

1 runs over the ball toward the defensive wall. 2 immediately passes the ball to 3. 3 lets the ball through to 5, while 4 serves as a decoy by running forward as the pass is made to 3. 5 shoots on goal.

CONTRIBUTOR: Karen S. Stanley, Assistant Women's Coach, University of Notre Dame, Notre Dame, Indiana

TRIANGULAR SERIES ▬▬▬▬▬▬▬

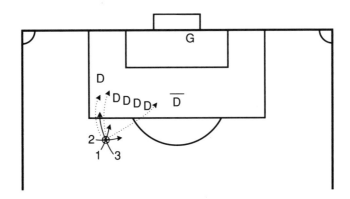

Formation

The ball is placed five yards outside the left side of the 18-yard line. Attackers 1, 2, and 3 are in position to take the free kick in a triangle formation, each player two feet from the ball.

Procedure

There are numerous shooting options from the starting formation. 1 chooses which option to implement. 1, 2, or 3 approach the ball as if to take a shot on goal. One or two players run over the ball, and one of the other players follows with a direct shot on goal. For indirect kicks, the players running over the ball move it no less than its circumference, and one of the other players follows with a shot on goal.

CONTRIBUTOR: John A. Reeves, Athletic Director, Columbia University, New York, New York

ULTRA CHALLENGE

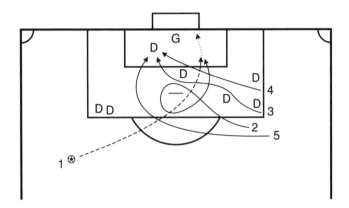

Formation
The ball is placed 30 yards from the goal line on the left side of the field. Attacker 1 is in position to take the free kick. Attackers 2, 3, 4, and 5 are spread out on the right side of the field.

Procedure
2 is the key figure in this restart. As 1 prepares for the kick, 2 sprints toward the near post. 1 does not pass the ball. 2 circles back out and around to the far post, moving slowly so as to not attract attention. 3, 4, and 5 then sprint to the near post. 1 passes the ball to the far post to 2, who shoots on goal.

CONTRIBUTORS: I.M. Ibrahim, Head Men's Coach, and Bob Winch, Assistant Men's Coach, Clemson University, Clemson, South Carolina

THE
CORNER KICK

In Part I we stressed the importance of preparing your team to act quickly and correctly in free kick situations. In the corner kick situation you have an added advantage—your team is in the area immediately in front of the goal being attacked. Should the opponents react slowly in setting up their defense, a successful corner kick could result from the same quick thinking and organization used in free kicks. However, because the defenders usually are in better positions than the attackers and outnumber the attackers in the goal area, a quick play is often counterproductive. Thus, it is better to take your time to set up a deliberate play.

In Part II we show you how to make the most of the corner kick advantage. Chapter 3 covers corner kick rules and prepares you to deal with the defense your team is likely to face. We explain important attacking principles and highlight specific player roles to help you select the best play and position key personnel.

Chapter 4 features the following 22 plays plus variations on those plays to provide excellent options for any corner kick situation. These plays are used by the country's top soccer programs when they want to score a corner kick goal. Use the helpful instructions and detailed diagrams to teach your team the plays. Add practice, and soon you'll be adding up the goals.

ATTACK
CLOCK
CORNER DRIVEN TO NEAR
  POST
CORNER ONE
CRASH
DOUBLE STACK
DRIVEN
FLICK ON
HEADING OPTIONS
IN AND OUT
LUNDY SKINNER
NATIONAL
NEAR OR FAR
OPEN UP
OVERLAP
PEEL OFF
SHOT
SIX
SOCCER POWER PLAY
STACK
TOPS
WEAKSIDE STAGGER RUNS

CHAPTER 3

CORNER KICK TACTICS

The corner kick offers great scoring opportunities because the ball is in the third of the field nearest your goal, and a goal can be scored directly from a corner kick. A corner kick is taken by a member of the attacking team to restart play after the ball has passed completely over the goal line (excluding the portion between the goalposts), either in the air or on the ground, having last been played by a member of the *defending* team.

RULES FOR THE CORNER KICK

 The attacking team restarts play by taking a kick from within the quarter circle at the nearest corner flagpost. The corner flag may not be removed during the corner kick.

 Defenders may not approach within 10 yards of the ball until the ball is in play, that is, until it has traveled the distance of its own circumference, or the kick shall be retaken.

 The kicker may not play the ball again until it has been touched or played by another player. Even if the ball hits the goalpost and rebounds toward the kicker, the kicker may not play the ball until it has been touched or played by another player.

Dealing With the Defense

When your team is awarded a corner kick, the defending team will already be within its defensive third of the field, and defensive players will move quickly, most likely to a partially prearranged defensive setup. Often, two defensive players will position themselves near the far post—one to protect the space behind the goalkeeper and the other to move out to cover an attacker who has occupied or is attempting to occupy vulnerable space. The goalkeeper will typically be close enough to the far post to be able to intercept a long cross to the far post or to move along the goal line or forward away from the goal line to catch balls that swing in toward the goal. A defender will probably be at the near post to clear a short kick from the goal area or to pass the ball to a teammate. Usually, another defender will be 10 yards from the player taking the corner kick to provide distraction and to be in position to intercept an errant cross or a pass to a nearby attacker. Other defensive players usually mark attacking players who have moved or may move to scoring positions. Defenders will try to create depth by positioning players from the goal line out to the middle third of the field so that a defender can clear or pass the ball immediately upfield to a teammate. Absence of defensive depth aids attacking players in regaining ball control as the defenders may be limited to making short passes in a confined area.

Attacking Principles

The attacking team enjoys the advantage of having the opportunity to execute well-rehearsed restart plays in the area immediately in front of the goal it is attacking.

Greater risk than usual may be taken by the attacking team in its final third of the field because even if the defending players gain possession, they must advance the ball almost the entire length of the field before creating a scoring opportunity of their own.

As emphasized during the discussion of the free kick, one player and alternates should be designated to signal by word or physical action (such as raising and dropping one arm) the start of the corner kick. Usually, it is convenient to have the player taking the corner kick give the signal. All attacking players, except the goalkeeper, have a role during the corner kick play, whether it is receiving the corner kick and shooting, receiving and passing, playing a "dummy" role such as allowing the ball to pass through the legs or over the head, or serving as a decoy to move a defensive player out of a particular area to provide space for the play. Finally, some attacking players should assume a defensive position to prevent a quick counterattack by the defending team.

CHAPTER 4

CORNER KICK PLAYS

The 22 corner kick restart plays in this chapter will provide you with numerous alternatives from which to select a few plays to rehearse and use in game situations. Plays can be made nearly perfect through practicing proper technique, communication, movement, and timing.

Typically, the player taking the corner kick or the coach will determine the play to be executed. You can use the following factors to choose the appropriate play:

- Defensive positions assumed by the opposing players
- Environmental conditions such as high wind, which may prompt the kicker to elect to keep the ball low or make a short pass, or slippery conditions, which may suggest that the kicker take a direct curved shot on goal
- Strengths and weaknesses of both attackers and defenders

KEY TO PLAY DIAGRAMS

D = *Defender*   〜〜〜➤ = **Dribble**

G = *Goalkeeper*   --------➤ = **Pass**

                       ⋯⋯⋯➤ = **Shot**

                       ————➤ = **Sprint**

                          ⊛ = **Ball**

ATTACK

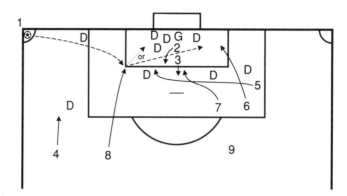

Formation
Attacker 1 is in position to take the corner kick. Attackers 2 and 3 are in the middle of the goal area. Attacker 4 is at the edge of the attacking third of the field, 10 yards in from the near sideline. Attackers 5, 6, and 7 are spread out inside the far corner of the penalty area. Attackers 8 and 9 are outside the near and far corners, respectively, of the 18-yard line.

Procedure
As soon as 1 gives the predetermined signal, 2 and 3 check to the six-yard line. 4 makes a delayed run toward the goal line. 5, 6, and 7 make delayed sprints to cover the near-post corner, far-post corner, and middle of the goal area, respectively. 1 makes an outswinger or inswinger corner kick to 8, who has sprinted toward the near corner of the goal area. 8 takes a first-time shot on goal or flicks the ball to the far post to 6, who takes a shot on goal. All other players stay alert for a possible rebound.

Variation

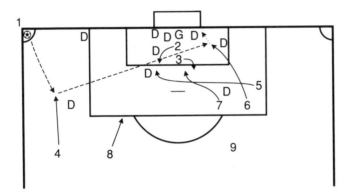

As soon as 1 gives the predetermined signal, 2 and 3 check to the six-yard line. 5, 6, and 7 make delayed sprints to cover the near-post corner, far-post corner, and middle of the goal area, respectively. 1 passes to 4, who is making a delayed run toward the goal line. 4 either goes two-on-one with 1 or crosses to the far post to 6, who shoots on goal.

CONTRIBUTOR: Thomas R. Martin, Men's Coach, James Madison University, Harrisonburg, Virginia

CLOCK

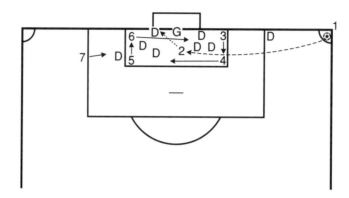

Formation

Attacker 1 is in position to take the corner kick. Attacker 2, who should be a tall player, is in the middle of the goal area. Attackers 3, 4, 5, and 6 are each in a different corner of the goal area. Attacker 7 is on the far sideline of the penalty area near the goal line.

Procedure

1 initiates the restart by yelling "Clock!" 3, 4, 5, and 6 immediately move clockwise around the inside of the goal area perimeter, keeping the spacing of their initial positions. 1 makes a high corner kick to 2, who takes a first-time head shot on goal. 3, 4, 5, and 6 stay alert for a possible rebound. 7 stays alert for a long corner kick or a loose ball slipping through the goal area.

Variation

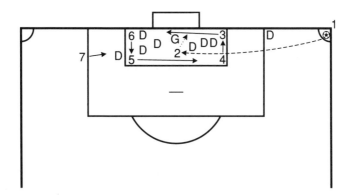

The kicker yells "Counter!" and the players move in a counterclockwise direction. The remainder of the play is completed as usual.

CONTRIBUTOR: Thomas M. Taylor, Boys' Coach, West Essex High School, North Caldwell, New Jersey

CORNER DRIVEN TO NEAR POST ▬▬▬▬

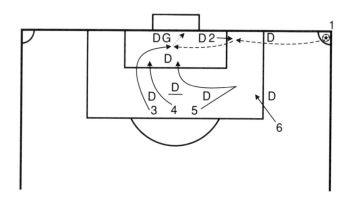

Formation
Attacker 1 is in position to take the corner kick. Attacker 2, preferably a tall player, is at the near post. Attackers 3, 4, and 5 stand along the top of the 18-yard line. Attacker 6 is just outside the 18-yard line on the same side as 1.

Procedure
On a predetermined signal, 3 makes a wide run past the far post toward the center of the goal area. 4 follows 3 and moves toward the far post. 5 checks toward 1 and then moves back toward the middle of the goal area. 6 moves to a position just inside the near sideline of the penalty area. 1 drives a head-high corner kick to 2, who moves toward the ball. 2 flicks the ball to the target area outside the far post for 3, who takes a first-time shot on goal. All other players stay alert for a possible rebound.

Variation

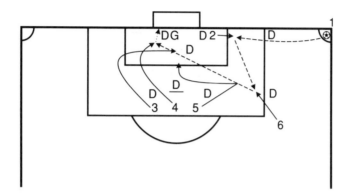

2, 3, 4, and 5 make the same runs. 1 drives the corner kick to 2. 2 heads the ball back to 6, who has moved into the penalty area. 6 crosses the ball first-time to the far post to 4, who takes a first-time shot on goal. All other players stay alert for a possible rebound.

CONTRIBUTOR: Diane R. Boettcher, Women's Coach, University of Maine, Orono, Maine

CORNER ONE

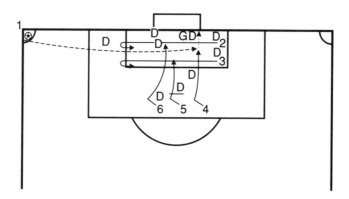

Formation

Attacker 1 is in position to take the corner kick. Attackers 2 and 3 are on the far sideline of the goal area. Attackers 4, 5, and 6 are in a line 15 yards from the goal line and parallel to the 18-yard line.

Procedure

To initiate the restart play and to distract the goalkeeper, 2 and 3 sprint across the goal area and curl back once they reach the near sideline of the goal area. 4, 5, and 6 check in the direction of 1 and then curl back toward the goal area—4 toward the far post, 5 to the middle, and 6 toward the near post. 4, as the main target, must make an effective feinting move to get open. 1 counts one second and makes the corner kick to 4, who takes a first-time shot on goal. All other attackers stay alert for a possible rebound.

Variation

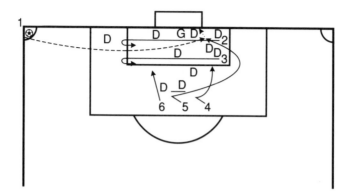

2 and 3 make the same runs. 4 and 5 check in the direction of 1. 4 then cuts to the right side of the goal area, and 5 cuts behind 4 and makes a far-post run. 6 moves forward toward the near-post area to be in position for a possible rebound. 1 makes the corner kick to 5 at the far post for a shot on goal.

CONTRIBUTOR: George D. Danner, Boys' Coach, Griffin High School, Griffin, Georgia

CRASH

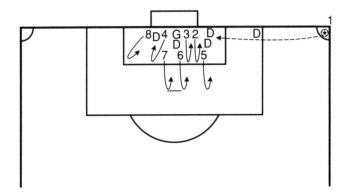

Formation
Attacker 1 is in position to take the corner kick. Attackers 2, 3, and 4 stand along the goal line within the goal area. Attackers 5, 6, and 7 stand behind 2, 3, and 4, respectively. Attacker 8 stands on the goal line at the far post.

Procedure
On a predetermined signal from 1, all attackers check away from their initial positions and then "crash" back toward the goal area. 2, 3, and 4 check to the six-yard line and move back toward the goal line. 5, 6, and 7 check back until they are even with the penalty line and then move back toward the goal area. 8 checks toward the six-yard line and then moves back to the far post. As the attackers are moving back, 1 makes a hard-driven corner kick to the near post to 2, who takes a first-time shot on goal or flicks the ball on to the far post for any open player to shoot on goal.

CONTRIBUTOR: Daniel Gilmore, Men's Coach, Rowan College of New Jersey, Glassboro, New Jersey

DOUBLE STACK

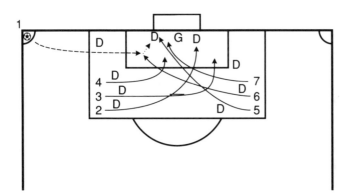

Formation
Attacker 1 is in position to take the corner kick. Two lines of three attackers each—Attackers 2, 3, and 4 and Attackers 5, 6, and 7—are at opposite sides of the penalty area.

Procedure
Just before making the corner kick, 1 calls out a number from 1 to 4 to indicate where he or she will kick the ball:

1—near post
2—far post
3—penalty line
4—center of goal area

The players in each line run toward predetermined positions:

Attacker 2—far post
Attacker 3—far-post corner of goal area
Attacker 4—middle of penalty area
Attacker 5—near post
Attacker 6—near-post corner of goal area
Attacker 7—in front of goalkeeper

The first player to contact the ball takes a first-time shot on goal. All other players keep alert for a possible rebound.

CONTRIBUTOR: Daniel R. Coombs, Boys' Coach, Loyola Academy, Wilmette, Illinois; Girls' Coach, Mother McAuley High School, Chicago, Illinois

DRIVEN

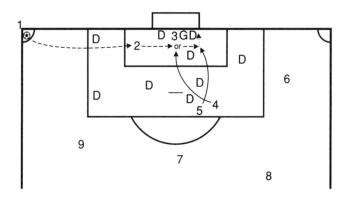

Formation
Attacker 1 is in position to take the corner kick. Attacker 2, who should be tall, is at the near corner of the goal area. Attacker 3 is in front of the goalkeeper. Attackers 4 and 5 are at the far side of the penalty area near the 18-yard line. Attackers 6, 7, 8, and 9 are spread out in the attacking third of the field.

Procedure
1 makes the corner kick to 2. 2 flicks the ball on to 5 or 4, who have made crisscrossing runs to the far post and the middle of the goal area, respectively. Whoever contacts the ball takes a first-time head volley shot on goal. 3 stays alert for a possible rebound. 6, 7, 8, and 9 maintain their positions, keeping alert for a possible long rebound or defensive clear.

Variation

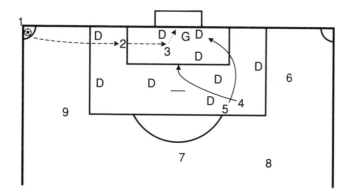

1 makes the corner kick to 2, who lets the ball run through to 3 for a first-time shot on goal. To get into position for a possible rebound, 4 and 5 make crisscrossing runs to the midpoint of the 6-yard line and far post, respectively.

CONTRIBUTOR: Michael C. Mooney, Men's Coach, State University of New York College at Geneseo, Geneseo, New York

FLICK ON

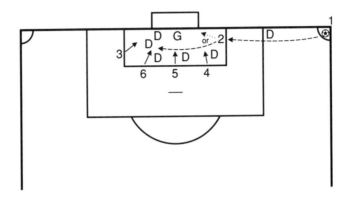

Formation
Attacker 1 is in position to take the corner kick. Attacker 2 is two yards from the goal line and two yards from the near post. Attacker 3 is on the far side of the six-yard line halfway between the goal line and the six-yard line. Attackers 4, 5, and 6 are in a line along the six-yard line.

Procedure
1 plays an air ball to 2's head. 2 can flick the ball on to goal, to 3 at the far post, or to 4, 5, or 6, who moved into the goal area as 1 made the corner kick. All players stay alert for a possible rebound.

CONTRIBUTOR: John Makuvek, Men's Coach, Moravian College, Bethlehem, Pennsylvania

HEADING OPTIONS

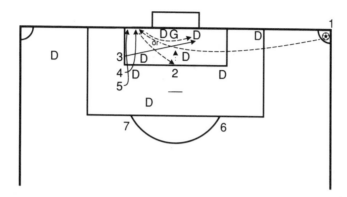

Formation

Attacker 1 is in position to take the corner kick. Attacker 2 stands on the center of the six-yard line. Attackers 3, 4, and 5 are in a line just outside the far corner of the six-yard line. Attackers 6 and 7 are on opposite ends of the penalty-area restraining arc.

Procedure

On a predetermined signal from 1, 3 sprints to the near post, 4 runs to the goal line midway between the far post and the perimeter of the goal area, and 5 runs to the end line at the far corner of the goal area. 1 drives a high ball to 4, who makes a head pass either to 2 in the middle of the goal area or to 3, who has turned around at the near post to look for the pass. The player who receives the pass takes a first-time shot on goal. The other players stay alert for a possible rebound. 6 and 7 stay alert for a possible long rebound or defensive clear.

CONTRIBUTOR: George Perry III, Men's Coach, St. Bonaventure University, St. Bonaventure, New York

IN AND OUT

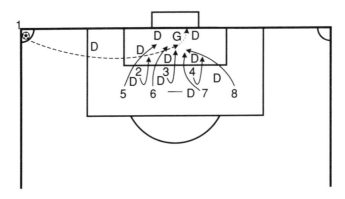

Formation

Attacker 1 is in position to take the corner kick. Attackers 2, 3, and 4 stand two yards apart from each other along the six-yard line. Attackers 5 and 6 stand two yards apart inside the left side of the penalty line. Attackers 7 and 8 stand two yards apart inside the right side of the penalty line.

Procedure

On a predetermined signal, the following happens simultaneously: 1 drives the corner kick toward the center of the goal area; 2, 3, and 4 take two steps out away from the goal line and then immediately run back in toward the goal area; 5 and 6 run toward the far post; and 7 and 8 run toward the near post. The first player to contact the ball takes a first-time shot on goal. All other players stay alert for a possible rebound.

Variation 1

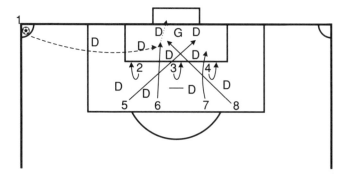

On a predetermined signal, the following happens simultaneously: 1 drives the corner kick toward the center of the goal area; 2, 3, and 4 move away from the goal area and turn back to positions just outside the goal area; 5 and 8 make crossover runs toward the far and near posts, respectively; and 6 and 7 make straight runs to the near and far posts, respectively. The first player to contact the ball takes a first-time shot on goal. All other players stay alert for a possible rebound.

Variation 2

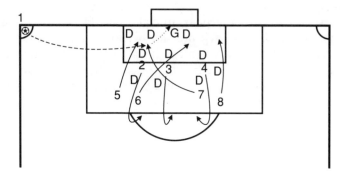

On a predetermined signal, the following happens simultaneously: 1 drives the corner kick toward the center of the goal area; 2, 3, and 4 move completely out of the penalty area and turn back to positions just outside the penalty area; 6 and 7 make crossover runs to the far and near posts, respectively; and 5 and 8 make straight runs to the near and far posts, respectively. The first player to contact the ball takes a first-time shot on goal. All other players stay alert for a possible rebound.

CONTRIBUTOR: Stephen G. Scullion, Boys' Coach, Folling Community Club, Tyne and Wear, England

LUNDY SKINNER

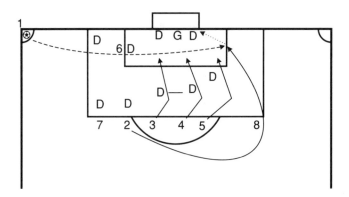

Formation

Attacker 1 is in position to take the corner kick. Attackers 2, 3, 4, and 5 stand from left to right along the top of the 18-yard line. Attacker 6 is on the near-post sideline of the goal area. Attackers 7 and 8 are just outside the near and far corners, respectively, of the 18-yard line.

Procedure

After 1 gives a predetermined signal, 3, 4, and 5 check away from 1 and then sprint toward the near, middle, and far areas of the goal area, respectively. 2 cuts back around 8 and sprints toward the far post. 1 drives the corner kick to the far post to 2, who takes a first-time shot on goal or flicks the ball back across the goal for any of the other attackers to shoot on goal. 7 and 8 maintain their positions and stay alert for possible defensive clears.

Variation

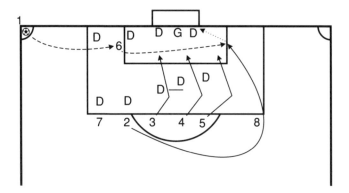

After 1 gives a predetermined signal, 3, 4, and 5 check away from 1 and then sprint toward the near, middle, and far areas of the goal area, respectively. 2 cuts back around 8 and sprints toward the far post. 1 makes a corner kick to 6, who flicks the ball on to 2 at the far post for a first-time shot on goal.

CONTRIBUTOR: Bob E. Warming, Men's Coach, Creighton University, Omaha, Nebraska

NATIONAL

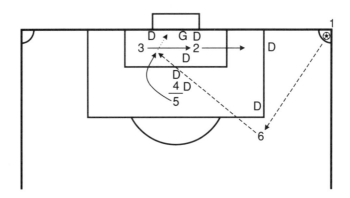

Formation

Attacker 1 is in position to take the corner kick. Attacker 2 is at the near post, and Attacker 3 is at the far post. Attacker 5 stands at the penalty line, and Attacker 4 stands in front of 5, a yard closer to the goal. Attacker 6, who should be a midfielder or fullback, is behind the corner of the 18-yard line on the same side of the field as 1.

Procedure

As 1 moves toward the ball to take the corner kick, 2, calling for the ball, sprints toward 1. 3 moves across to the near post. 1 makes a well-paced ground ball pass to 6, who makes a one-touch pass toward the far post. In order for the pass to move in a downward arc, 6 should make the pass with the inside of the instep. 5, who has sprinted to the far post to receive the pass, shoots on goal. 3 and 4 stay alert for a possible rebound.

Variation

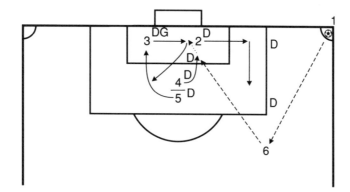

If the defense moves out of the penalty area on the pass from 1 to 6, 2 and 3 sprint away from the goal line to keep in onside positions. 4 and 5 move to the near post and far post, respectively, as 6 passes to either player for a one-time shot on goal.

CONTRIBUTOR: Helmut Werner, Men's Coach, Randolph-Macon College, Ashland, Virginia

NEAR OR FAR

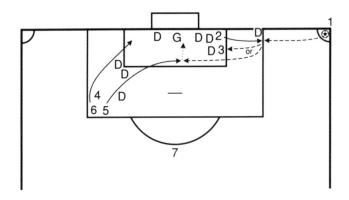

Formation

Attacker 1 is in position to take the corner kick. Attackers 2 and 3 are at the near corner of the goal area. Attackers 4, 5, and 6 are next to each other at the far corner of the penalty area. Attacker 7 is at the midpoint of the penalty-area restraining arc.

Procedure

On a predetermined signal from 1, 2 runs toward the near sideline of the penalty area. 1 makes the corner kick to 2's head. 5 sprints to the middle of the goal area, and 6 sprints toward the far post. 2 flicks to 3 or 5. Whoever contacts the ball takes a first-time shot on goal. 6 stays alert for a possible rebound or a further flick from 5. 4 and 7 stay alert for a possible long rebound or defensive clear.

Variation

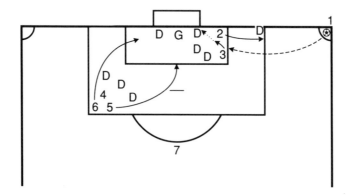

On a predetermined signal from 1, 2 runs toward the near sideline of the penalty area, 5 sprints to the middle of the goal area, and 6 sprints toward the far post. 1 makes the corner kick to 3, who turns inside and shoots first-time on goal. All other attackers stay alert for a possible rebound or defensive clear.

CONTRIBUTOR: Jeffrey R. Tipping, Men's Coach, Muhlenberg College, Allentown, Pennsylvania

OPEN UP

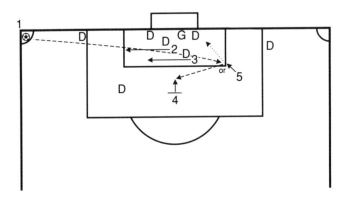

Formation

Attacker 1 is in position to take the corner kick. Attacker 2 is in the center of the goal area. Attacker 3 is near the far corner of the six-yard line. Attacker 4 is on the penalty line. Attacker 5 is two yards outside the far corner of the six-yard line.

Procedure

After 1 gives a predetermined signal, 2 and 3 sprint toward the near sideline of the penalty area. 1 makes an outswinger corner kick to the far corner of the six-yard line to 5, who has timed a sprint to meet the ball as it gets to the corner. 5 either shoots first-time on goal or passes across the middle to 4, who has sprinted toward goal from the penalty line to be in position to receive the pass and take a shot on goal.

CONTRIBUTOR: Jay Martin, Men's Coach, Ohio Wesleyan University, Delaware, Ohio

OVERLAP

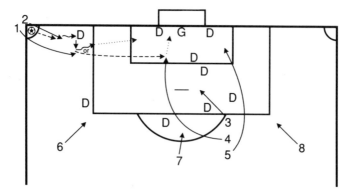

Formation
Attackers 1 and 2 are in position to take the corner kick. Attackers 3, 4, and 5 form a line parallel to the sideline near the far end of the 18-yard line. Attackers 6, 7, and 8 are spread out a few yards outside the 18-yard line from left to right, respectively.

Procedure
1 initiates the play by tapping the ball forward to 2. 2 attacks and isolates a defender. 1 overlaps and receives a pass from 2. As 1 overlaps 2, 4 sprints toward the near post, 5 sprints toward the far post, and 3 sprints toward the penalty line. 1 either dribbles toward the goal and shoots to the near post or passes to 4, who takes a first-time shot on goal. 3 and 5 keep alert for a possible rebound. 6, 7, and 8, who have moved in toward the penalty area, stay alert for a possible long rebound or clear.

CONTRIBUTOR: TJ Kostecky, Men's Coach, New Jersey Institute of Technology, Newark, New Jersey

PEEL OFF

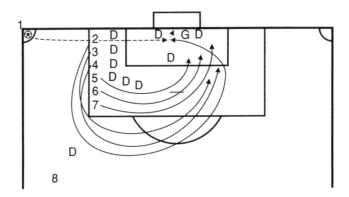

Formation
Attacker 1 is in position to take the corner kick. Six attackers, Attackers 2 to 7, line up on the penalty area sideline nearest 1. Attacker 8 stands 10 yards in from the near sideline and about 30 yards from the goal line.

Procedure
On a predetermined signal from 1, the attacking players, beginning with 7, peel off one after the other and make bending sequential runs toward the far-post area. 2 continues to the near-post area. 1 makes a low corner kick to the near post to 2, who shoots on goal. All other attackers stay alert for a possible rebound.

Variation

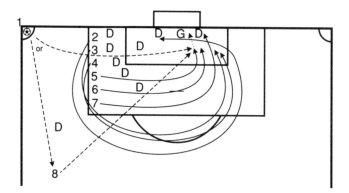

On a predetermined signal from 1, the attacking players, beginning with 7, peel off one after the other and make bending sequential runs toward the far-post area. 2 continues to the near-post area. 1 makes the corner kick to the far post or passes to 8, who crosses the ball to the far post. The first player to contact the ball at the far post takes a first-time shot on goal.

CONTRIBUTOR: C. Cliff McCrath, Men's Coach, Seattle Pacific University, Seattle, Washington

SHOT

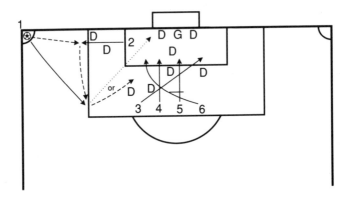

Formation

Attacker 1 is in position to take the corner kick. Attacker 2 is at the near-post corner of the goal area. Attackers 3, 4, 5, and 6 stand from left to right along the top of the 18-yard line.

Procedure

1 initiates the corner kick by giving a predetermined signal to 2. 2 moves toward 1. 1 plays a short ball to 2 at the penalty area sideline. 1 follows the pass with a run toward the top of penalty area sideline and receives a pass back from 2. As 2 makes the pass, the attackers on the 18-yard line sprint into the goal area, with 3 and 6 crisscrossing to the far and near posts, respectively, and 4 and 5 making straight runs. 1 either takes a shot on goal or passes to one of the attackers in the goal area, who takes a shot on goal. All other attackers stay alert for a possible rebound.

Variation

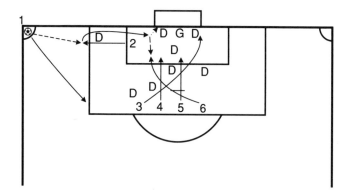

1 initiates the corner kick by giving a predetermined signal to 2. 2 moves toward 1. 1 plays a short ball to 2 at the penalty area sideline. If 2's defender is loosely marking or moves to cut off 2's pass to 1, 2 turns toward the goal line and shoots on goal or makes a short corner kick to the other attackers moving in on goal. The first player to contact the ball takes a first-time shot on goal. All other attackers stay alert for a possible rebound.

CONTRIBUTOR: Nick Mykulak, Men's Coach, Stevens Institute of Technology, Hoboken, New Jersey

SIX

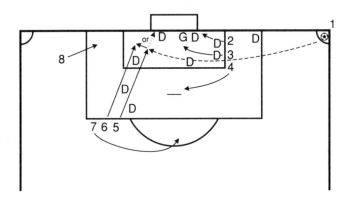

Formation

Attacker 1 is in position to take the corner kick. Attackers 2, 3, and 4 stand along the near-post sideline of the goal area. Attackers 5, 6, and 7 are in a line along the far side of the 18-yard line. Attacker 8 is 10 yards outside the far sideline of the penalty area and several yards in from the goal line.

Procedure

The object of this restart is to get the ball to the feet of 5 or 6 at the far post. Well-timed decoy runs by the other attackers to clear space and confuse the defense are essential to this restart's success. As 1 moves into position to take the corner kick, 2 cuts inside to the near post, 3 moves inside to the middle of the goal area, and 4 spins inside to the middle of the penalty area. As 1 makes a strong, low corner kick to the far post, 5 and 6 sprint toward the far post with 6 just a few yards behind 5. 5 takes a first-time shot on goal or dummies the ball to 6, who shoots on goal. 2 and 3 stay alert for a possible short rebound. 7 and 8 move into position to be ready for a possible long rebound or clear.

Variation

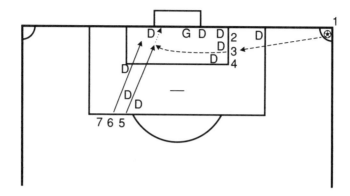

2, 3, and 4 maintain their positions. 5 and 6 sprint toward the far post. 1 serves a head-high ball toward 2, 3, and 4, and one of them flicks the ball to the far post for a head shot on goal by either 5 or 6. All other attackers stay alert for a possible rebound or clear.

CONTRIBUTOR: Brian J. Woods, Men's Coach, William Paterson College of New Jersey, Wayne, New Jersey

SOCCER POWER PLAY

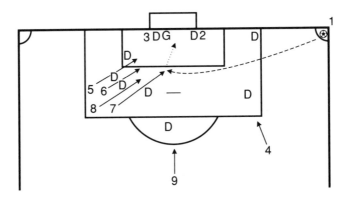

Formation

Attacker 1 is in position to take the corner kick. Attackers 2 and 3 are at the near and far posts, respectively. Attacker 4 stands a few yards outside the near corner of the penalty area. Attackers 5, 6, 7, and 8 are in echelon formation at the far corner of the penalty area. Attacker 9 stands 10 yards outside the midpoint of the penalty-area restraining arc.

Procedure

As 1 attempts a seven-foot-high corner kick to an area two yards outside the middle of the goal area, 5, 6, 7, and 8 sprint toward the ball to get a first-time head or kick shot on goal. 2 and 3 stay alert for a short or long corner or rebound. 4 and 9 stay alert to redirect clears or rebounds back toward goal.

CONTRIBUTOR: John A. Reeves, Athletic Director, Columbia University, New York, New York

STACK

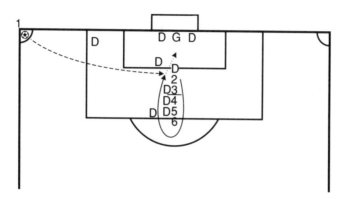

Formation

Attacker 1 is in position to take the corner kick. Attackers 2, 3, 4, 5, and 6 form a line parallel to the sideline in the center of the penalty area and face 1.

Procedure

2 initiates the restart by running around the end of the stack of attackers and then forward to meet the corner kick served by 1 toward the far post. 2 shoots on goal toward the near post.

CONTRIBUTOR: Susan M. Ryan, Women's Coach, State University of New York at Stony Brook, Stony Brook, New York

TOPS

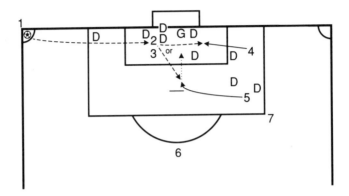

Formation

Attacker 1 is in position to take the corner kick. Attackers 2 and 3 stand shoulder-to-shoulder at the near post. Attacker 4 stands near the far sideline of the penalty area, and Attacker 5 stands inside the far top corner of the penalty area. Attacker 7 is a few yards behind 5 outside the far corner of the penalty area. Attacker 6 is at the midpoint of the penalty-area restraining arc.

Procedure

1 serves a low hard-driven ball to the near post. 4 runs to the far post area, and 5 runs to the penalty line. 2 flicks the ball to either 4 or 5, and whoever contacts the ball takes a head or volley shot on goal. 6 and 7 hold their positions outside the penalty area and stay alert for possible long rebounds or clears.

CONTRIBUTOR: Vernon H. Mummert, Men's Coach, Drew University, Madison, New Jersey

WEAKSIDE STAGGER RUNS

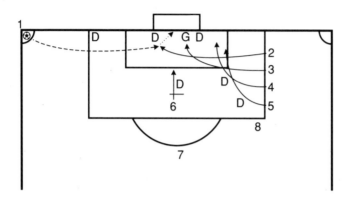

Formation
Attacker 1 is in position to take the corner kick. Attackers 2, 3, 4, and 5 are in a line on the far sideline of the penalty area. Attacker 6 stands on the penalty line. Attacker 7 is at the midpoint of the penalty-area restraining arc.

Procedure
On a predetermined signal from 1, the four attackers on the penalty area sideline, beginning with 2, make sequential runs for designated areas: 2 to the near post, 3 toward the goalkeeper, 4 to the far post, and 5 to a position at the far-post area just a few yards behind 4. 6 moves to the middle of the goal area. 1 drives a low corner kick, timing it to arrive at the near post at the same time as 2. 2 takes a first-time shot on goal. 3, 4, 5, and 6 stay alert for a possible rebound. 7 stays alert for a possible long rebound or clear.

CONTRIBUTOR: Ted Eskildsen, Women's Coach, Grinnell College, Grinnell, Iowa

THE THROW-IN AND KICKOFF

As with the free kick and the corner kick, the throw-in and kickoff offer offenses the opportunity to move into attacking positions either by exploiting a slow-reacting defense with a quick play or by moving to predetermined positions designed to gain a tactical advantage. Quickness is generally effective in throw-in plays, but there is obviously no need to rush the kickoff play.

In Part III we show you how to make the most of throw-in and kickoff plays. In chapter 5 we outline throw-in and kickoff rules and describe what kind of defenses to anticipate. We discuss attacking principles including what roles your players might fill. In chapter 6 you'll find the following eight throw-in and two kickoff restarts and additional variations to strengthen your team's play in these situations.

Throw-In Plays

CLEAR SPACE INTO SPACE
FILLER
FLICK ON TO GOAL
POWER
SCISSORS
SOCCER LINE GO
THROW TO SCORE
TOP FLICK

Kickoff Plays

QUICK OPENER
WEAVE

CHAPTER 5

THROW-IN AND KICKOFF TACTICS

The throw-in and kickoff both occur in deadball situations to either start or restart play at the beginning of the game, after a score in the case of the kickoff, or when the ball has gone out-of-bounds in the case of the throw-in.

RULES FOR THE THROW-IN

 A throw-in is taken to return the ball to play after it has passed completely over a sideline (touchline).

 The thrower, at the moment he or she is delivering the ball, must face the field of play, and part of each foot must be either on the sideline or on the ground outside the sideline. The thrower must use both hands equally, and must throw the ball from behind and over his or her head. The throw-in is taken from the point where the ball crossed the sideline. Any player on the team opposite to that of the player who last touched the ball can throw in the ball. The ball is in play as soon as it enters the field. A goal may not be scored directly from a throw-in.

 If the ball is not properly thrown in as described, a throw-in will be taken by a player of the opposing team.

The thrower, as is the case with the kicker of free and corner kicks, cannot play the ball again until it has been touched or played by another player.

RULES FOR THE KICKOFF

 A kickoff is held to start play at the beginning of a game, and to restart play in the second half, for any overtime periods, and after a goal is scored. The kickoff is made by kicking a ball that is stationary on the ground in the center of the field into the opponent's half of the field. Every player must be in his or her half of the field, and every player of the team opposing the kicker must be at least 10 yards from the ball until it is kicked off. A ball is kicked off when it travels forward at least the distance of its circumference. A goal may not be scored directly from a kickoff. As with all restarts, the kicker may not play the ball again until it has been touched or played by another player.

Dealing With the Defense

A throw-in taken in the attacking half of the field is dangerous for the defense, because the team in control of the ball may use a set play and because a player cannot be offside on the throw-in. Attacking teams should use this danger to their advantage. Conversely, throw-ins taken in the attacker's defensive third of the field actually may provide the defensive team with a scoring opportunity. Therefore, the attacking team must play with extreme caution in this area.

During a throw-in, defenders will mark attacking players and space. Defenders are particularly vulnerable to being beaten by a move to the ball followed by a sprint behind the defender to space or to goal and by a long throw to space when defenders are closely marking attackers. Even more dangerous to the defense is a throw to space immediately in front of the goal.

At the kickoff, the offensive team should not allow the defenders the opportunity to get a psychological advantage by gaining possession. This is particularly true if possession is regained by a team that has just scored a goal. To maximize the possibility of regaining the ball, defenders will anticipate where the ball will be passed and react quickly to cut off passing lanes.

Attacking Principles

The attacking team has a distinct advantage during the throw-in because it can plan various plays such as those in chapter 6. Attackers may move quickly to the goal they are facing, while defenders have the disadvantages of moving backwards and having to anticipate the attacker's plans. Each attacking player has a role in the throw-in, such as receiving the ball from the thrower and then shooting or passing, or serving as a decoy to create space for another player.

There are two basic, but different, attack objectives for the kickoff. One is to accomplish quick and deep penetration into the final third of the field that will put immediate pressure on the defense and create a scoring opportunity. The other is to retain possession of the ball, giving team players confidence early in the game.

CHAPTER 6

THROW-IN AND KICKOFF PLAYS

The eight throw-in restart plays in this chapter will provide you with an arsenal of plays to accommodate most throw-in situations.

Some teams may choose not to use a set kickoff play, opting instead to develop spontaneous play from the field. Two kickoff plays are presented for those of you who wish to have a set plan for this situation.

KEY TO PLAY DIAGRAMS

D = *Defender*

G = *Goalkeeper*

〜〜〜➤ = **Dribble**

------➤ = **Pass**

·············➤ = **Shot**

————➤ = **Sprint**

⊛ = **Ball**

CLEAR SPACE INTO SPACE ━━━━━━━

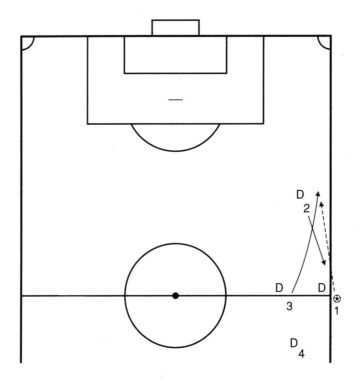

Formation

Attacker 1 is in position to take the throw-in at midfield. Attacker 2 stands near the sideline 20 yards closer to the goal line. Attacker 3 is square with 1 and 10 yards away from 1. Attacker 4 is behind 3 and 10 yards farther away from the goal line.

Procedure

2 initiates the throw-in by running toward 1. 3 sprints toward the space vacated by 2, timing the run to receive the throw-in from 1. 1 throws into the area between 3 and the sideline so that 3 can receive the ball on the run and shield it from the defender.

Variation 1

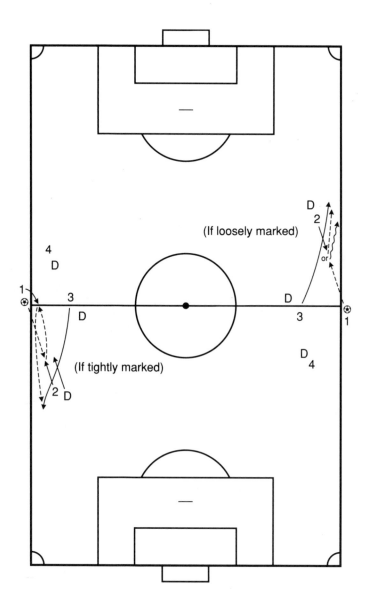

2 runs toward 1. 1 makes the throw-in to 2. If loosely marked, 2 turns with the ball and either moves upfield or passes to 3, who has run to the space vacated by 2. If tightly marked, 2 passes back to 1, who enters the field immediately after making the throw-in. 1 then passes the ball upfield to 3.

Variation 2

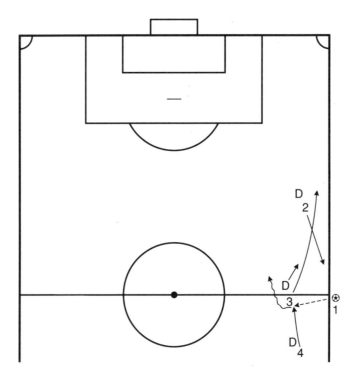

2 runs toward 1. 3 runs to the space vacated by 2, and, at the same time, 4 runs to the space vacated by 3. 1 makes a square throw-in to 4, who moves upfield with the ball.

CONTRIBUTOR: Jay Gavitt, Assistant Boys' Coach, Columbia High School, Maplewood, New Jersey

FILLER

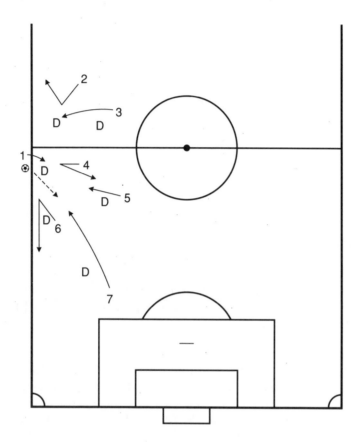

Formation

Attacker 1 is in position to take the throw-in near midfield. Attackers 2, 4, and 6 and Attackers 3, 5, and 7 form two wide arcs, one behind the other, facing 1.

Procedure

2 and 3, 4 and 5, and 6 and 7 work as partners. 2, 4, and 6 check toward 1 and then move away at varying times. When these players move away, 3, 5, and 7 move into the space vacated by each partner. 1 throws in to any of the attackers and immediately moves onto the field to support further play.

CONTRIBUTOR: Shawn Ladda, Women's Coach, Columbia University, New York, New York

FLICK ON TO GOAL

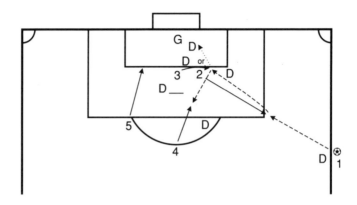

Formation

Attacker 1 is in position to take the throw-in 25 yards from the goal line. Attacker 3 stands on the midpoint of the six-yard line. Attacker 2 is five yards closer to the near sideline than 3. Attacker 4 stands on the midpoint of the penalty-area restraining arc. Attacker 5 is 10 yards to the left of 4.

Procedure

2 initiates the throw-in by running toward 1. 1 throws to the head of 2. 2 flicks toward goal to 3, who has moved to the space vacated by 2. 3 turns and either shoots on goal or passes to 4, who has run toward the goal area to be in position to receive the pass or to handle a possible rebound if 3 shoots on goal. 5 moves toward the goal area to be in position for a possible rebound.

Variation

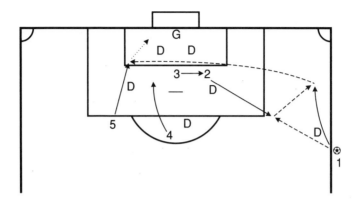

2 initiates the throw-in by running toward 1. As 3 moves to the space vacated by 2, 1 throws to the head of 2. 2 heads the ball toward the corner to 1, who enters the field immediately after the throw-in. 1, who has moved toward the goal line, crosses the ball to 5, who takes a first-time shot on goal. 4 moves toward the goal area to be in position for a possible rebound.

CONTRIBUTORS: Anson Dorrance, Head Women's Coach, and Bill Palladino, Assistant Women's Coach, University of North Carolina, Chapel Hill, North Carolina

POWER

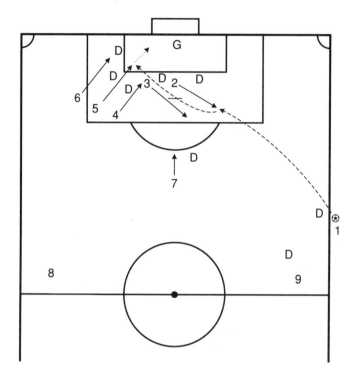

Formation
Attacker 1 is in position to take a throw-in 30 yards from the goal line. Attackers 2 and 3, two tall players, are just outside the six-yard line, five yards apart. Attackers 4, 5, and 6 are in a line on the far side of the penalty area. Attacker 7 is several yards outside the midpoint of the penalty-area restraining arc. Attackers 8 and 9 are at wide positions opposite each other in the attacking side of the field, near the midfield line.

Procedure
1 makes a long throw-in to 2 or 3, who have moved toward the ball but kept their spacing. 2 or 3 flicks the ball to 4, 5, or 6, who must anticipate the pass and run to the ball. The first player to contact the ball takes a first-time shot on goal. 7 moves toward the top of the penalty-area restraining arc to be in position for a possible rebound or clear.

Variation

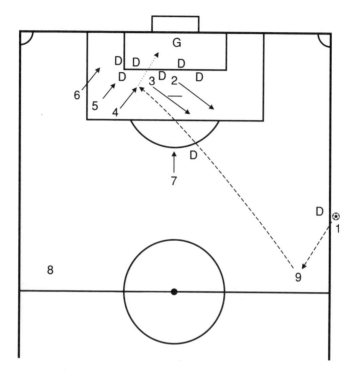

2 and 3 move toward 1 but keep their spacing. If the defense sags in to cover the long throw-in, 1 throws in to 9, who crosses the ball to the far post to 4, 5, or 6, who shoots on goal.

CONTRIBUTOR: Brian E. Chafin, Men's Coach, Centre College, Danville, Kentucky

SCISSORS

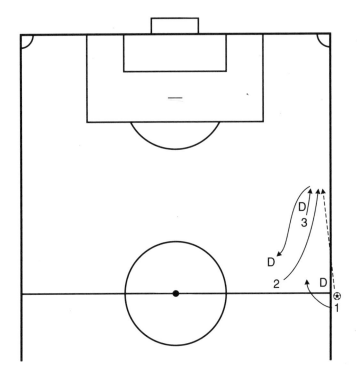

Formation
Attacker 1 is in position to take the throw-in at midfield. Attacker 2 lines up square to and 15 yards from 1. Attacker 3 is 15 yards down the line from 1.

Procedure
3 initiates the throw-in by moving down the line away from 1. 3 then turns and sprints toward the defender marking 2. At the same time, 2 makes a run toward the space vacated by 3. (The play is designed to lose 2's defender in the "traffic" created by the runs of 2 and 3. Therefore, it is important that 3 runs toward 2's defender and not 2.) 1, after faking first to 2's initial position inside, throws the ball down the line to 2 and immediately enters the field to support further play.

CONTRIBUTOR: Nick D. Sansom, Men's Coach, State University of New York at Stony Brook, Stony Brook, New York

SOCCER LINE GO

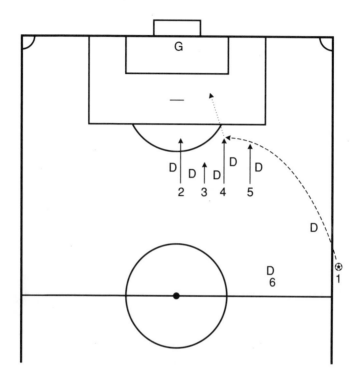

Formation
Attacker 1 is in position to take the throw-in near midfield. Attackers 2, 3, 4, and 5 are in a line from left to right, 15 yards outside the right side of the 18-yard line. Attacker 6 is at midfield, 10 yards from 1.

Procedure
On a predetermined signal, 2, 3, 4, and 5 sprint to the open space past their defenders. 1 makes the throw-in to this open space for any attacker to control and shoot on goal.

CONTRIBUTOR: John A. Reeves, Athletic Director, Columbia University, New York, New York

THROW TO SCORE

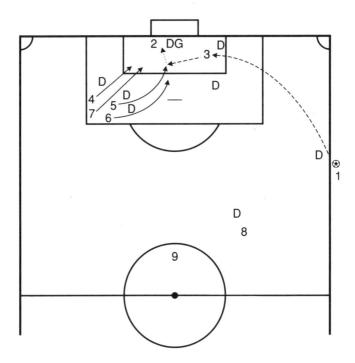

Formation

Attacker 1 is in position to take the throw-in 20 yards from the goal line. Attackers 2 and 3 are at the far and near posts, respectively. Attackers 4, 5, 6, and 7 are in an echelon formation at the far corner of the penalty area. Attackers 8 and 9 are near midfield, about 10 yards apart.

Procedure

1 throws toward the far or near post for 2 or 3. Whoever contacts the ball either shoots directly on goal or deflects the ball back toward 4, 5, 6, and 7, who are charging toward the goal area. Whoever contacts the ball takes a shot on goal. The others stay alert for a possible rebound.

Variation

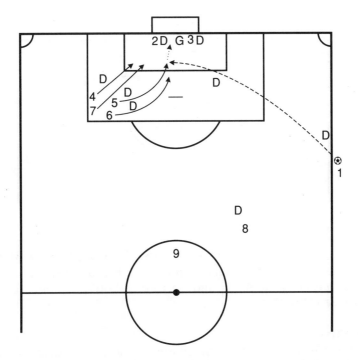

1 throws to the space between the echelon and the goalkeeper as the players in the echelon are moving toward the goal. The first player to contact the ball takes a first-time shot on goal.

CONTRIBUTOR: John A. Reeves, Athletic Director, Columbia University, New York, New York

TOP FLICK

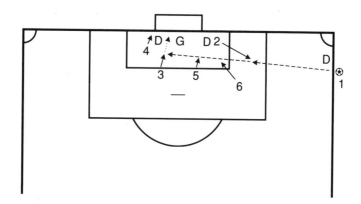

Formation

Attacker 1 is in position to take the throw-in 10 yards from the corner of the field. Attackers 2 and 4 stand at the near post and far post, respectively. Attackers 3, 5, and 6 are spread out in a line just outside the six-yard line.

Procedure

2 sprints toward a predetermined area outside the near corner of the goal area. 1 throws the ball to 2's head. 2 flicks the ball toward 3, 4, 5, or 6, who are sprinting toward predetermined positions. The first player to contact the ball takes a first-time shot on goal.

CONTRIBUTOR: Tom G. McLoughlin, Men's Coach, Fairleigh Dickinson University, Madison, New Jersey

QUICK OPENER

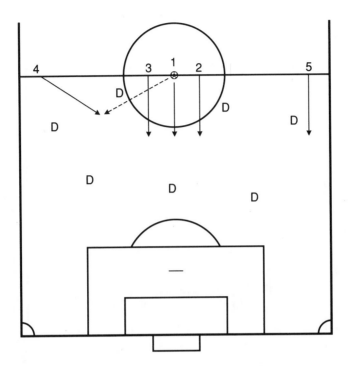

Formation
Attackers 1, 2, and 3 are in position to take the kickoff. Attackers 4 and 5 are on the right and left sides, respectively, of the midfield line.

Procedure
1 passes directly to 4, who cuts diagonally between defenders to receive the pass. 4 looks first to pass the ball to any attacker on a breakaway, but he or she may charge toward the goal or veer out to the sideline and down the wing. The other attackers move forward immediately after the pass.

Variation 1

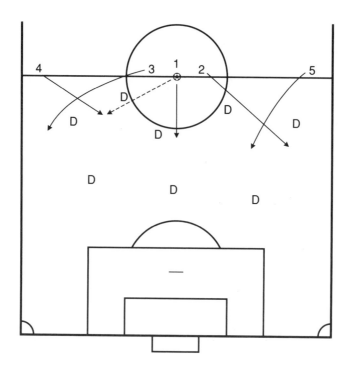

1 passes directly to 4, who cuts diagonally forward between defenders to receive the pass. On the pass, 3 cuts behind 4 and moves down the sideline. 1 sprints straight forward. 2 and 5 move diagonally forward and interchange positions. On receiving the pass, 4 looks first to pass to any attacker on a breakaway, but he or she may charge toward the goal, pass the ball out to either wing, or work a give and go with 1.

Variation 2

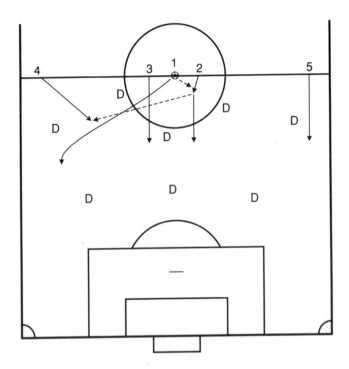

1 kicks off to 2, who moves diagonally forward to receive the pass. Following the kickoff, 1 cuts diagonally forward to an advance wing position on the right sideline. 2 passes to 4, who has cut diagonally forward between defenders to receive the pass. After 2's pass, 2, 3, and 5 sprint straight forward. On receiving the pass, 4 looks first to pass to any attacker on a breakaway, but he or she may charge toward the goal, pass the ball out to either wing, or work a give and go with 3.

CONTRIBUTOR: J. Malcolm Simon, Director of Physical Education and Athletics, New Jersey Institute of Technology, Newark, New Jersey

WEAVE

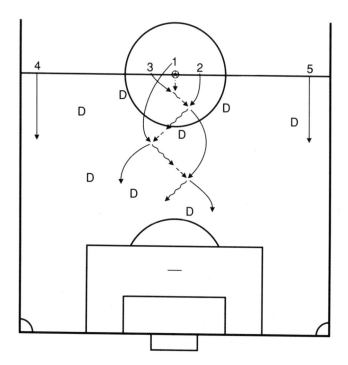

Formation
Attackers 1, 2, and 3 are in position to take the kickoff. Attackers 4 and 5 are on the right and left sides, respectively, of the midfield line.

Procedure
1 kicks off to 3, who moves diagonally forward to receive the pass. As 3 dribbles diagonally forward, 1 runs behind 3. 3 passes to 2, who reverses the diagonal dribble movement and passes to 1, who has cut to receive the pass. Play continues in this weave fashion until any of the players can execute a breakthrough. 4 and 5 make straight runs down the wing, keeping wide positions.

CONTRIBUTOR: J. Malcolm Simon, Director of Physical Education and Athletics, New Jersey Institute of Technology, Newark, New Jersey

ABOUT THE EDITORS

Malcolm Simon   John Reeves

Malcolm Simon and John Reeves combine more than 50 years of soccer coaching expertise in their newest coaches guide, *Soccer Restart Plays*. Two of America's top coaches, Simon and Reeves are the editors of three other highly acclaimed Human Kinetics soccer books: *Select Soccer Drills*, *Coaches Collection of Soccer Drills*, and *The Soccer Games Book*.

Malcolm Simon is the director of physical education and athletics at the New Jersey Institute of Technology. He has coached soccer, basketball, tennis, and volleyball in college, camp, and YMCA settings since 1954. His teams include NAIA national champions and runners-up. Sixteen of his players have been named All-Americans, and five have gone on to play professional soccer nationally and internationally, including Hernan "Chico" Borja. Simon is a member of the National Soccer Coaches Association of America and the Intercollegiate Soccer Association of America.

John Reeves has been coaching soccer since 1961 at both the youth and collegiate levels. Currently the director of intercollegiate athletics and physical education at Columbia University, Reeves is a member of the National Soccer Coaches Association of America and is past-president of the Intercollegiate Soccer Association of America. He was twice named New Jersey Soccer Coach of the Year. Dr. Reeves earned his doctoral degree in 1983 from Columbia University.